ELECTIO

THE INSIDE STORY OF
THE CAMPAIGN

Nicholas Jones

BBC Books

Picture credits (between text pages 80 and 81)
BBC page 5;
Camera Press 1, 3 (top);
Express Newspapers Plc 6 (lower left);
Financial Times/Tony Andrews 7 (top);
Katz/Richard Baker 2 (bg), 8, Andrew Moore 2 (top right);
Press Association 2 (top left), 3 (lower), 4 (top), 4 (lower), 5 (lower);
Rex Features 6 (top left and right), 7 (lower).

Published by BBC Books,
a division of BBC Enterprises Limited,
Woodlands, 80 Wood Lane
London W12 0TT

First published 1992

© Nicholas Jones 1992

ISBN 0 563 36124 7

Designed by David Robinson
Set in Century Old Style
Typeset by Ace Filmsetting Ltd, Frome
Printed and bound in Great Britain by
Clays Ltd, St Ives Plc
Cover printed by Clays Ltd, St Ives Plc

CONTENTS

ABOUT THE AUTHOR

Nicholas Jones is a BBC political correspondent and broadcasts regularly from Westminster for radio and television. He has been with the BBC for 20 years and during his career has specialised in reporting political and trade-union affairs.

He started in journalism in 1960 at the age of 17 and worked on local newspapers and on *The Times* before joining the BBC in 1972. In 1979 he was appointed labour correspondent for BBC Radio and spent most of the following decade covering the major industrial disputes of the Thatcher years, including the 1984–85 miners' strike. His first book, *Strikes and the Media*, was published by Basil Blackwell in 1986.

Nicholas Jones has had prior first-hand experience of general election reporting. In 1970 he was assigned by *The Times* to cover the campaign of the shadow foreign secretary, Sir Alec Douglas-Home, and in 1979 he followed Liberal leader David Steel.

INTRODUCTION

In the months leading up to the 1992 general election, the Conservatives and Labour were neck and neck in the opinion polls. As polling day approached many of the opinion polls put Labour slightly ahead. There was widespread expectation that the Conservatives could not remain the largest party. A hung parliament was the most popular prediction.

In the event, Mr Major confounded the pollsters *and* faint hearts in his own party, by achieving an overall majority of 21 in the newly elected House of Commons. The Conservatives won 336 seats with a 42.8% share of the vote. Labour's failure to match the promise of their campaign was a great disappointment to the party. Nevertheless Labour did succeed in defeating the Conservatives in 44 constituencies, taking their total number of seats to 271 with a 35.2% share of the vote. Twenty Liberal Democrat MPs were returned to parliament and their party gained 18.3% of the vote. All the other parties, including the Scottish Nationalists, Plaid Cymru and the Ulster parties, netted 24 seats, with a 3.7% share of the vote.

My diary follows the twists and turns of the campaign, from Mr Major's declaration of the election in mid-March, through to polling day on 9 April, and then on to the sudden resignation of the Labour leader Neil Kinnock.

To begin with I concentrate on the unsuccessful efforts of the Conservatives to break free from Labour and build up an opinion poll lead. Mr Major was an untried election campaigner. The political precedents were against him and the prospect of a change in government kept the focus firmly on the Tories. However, as the campaign develops, I devote more of my diary to the election tactics of Labour and the Liberal Democrats.

As a political correspondent employed by the BBC my job was to work mainly at Westminster, reporting and assessing the election for radio news bulletins. I was able to observe the political parties at close quarters and in addition to my daily broadcasts I kept a detailed note of what I heard and saw.

Much of what I reproduce is straight forward reportage: my own narrative of the unfolding campaign drawn from daily news conferences, speeches and interviews. However, I also include numerous quotations from politicians and party workers. Almost all of them are directly attributed. Many of these observations are from those party officials whose job it was to brief the news media and who usually prefer their work to remain anonymous. However, I consider that by placing their remarks in strict time and date chronology I give a fascinating insight into the fluctuating fortunes of the political parties.

All journalists think carefully before revealing the identity of their sources. My belief, as a political correspondent, is that once a campaign is over no politician nor party worker who has a direct interest in the outcome of the election should have any objection to conversations with journalists being subjected to retrospective analysis and assessment. I have sought to do that fairly and honestly.

Much of what was said to me during the campaign was inevitably omitted from my broadcasts. My task was to follow the events of the day and then compress them into short reports. There was little space in which to assess the course of the campaign.

I readily acknowledge that in the heat of political battle, when journalists are desperate for guidance, we have to accept that much of the information which we are given for immediate use is off-the-record. Conversations are regularly conducted only on that basis.

Political correspondents at Westminster follow well established conventions when attending lobby briefings in the House of Commons and in Downing Street: these are designed to prevent direct attribution. When parliament is sitting, conversations in the members' lobby are also considered off-the-record unless an MP states otherwise.

However throughout the election campaign, the news conferences or briefings which I attended were not held on lobby terms. Many of the discussions I had with politicians and party workers were in the presence of other journalists or were conducted by telephone. It is my belief that the information I record in my diary was given freely to a working journalist in the knowledge that it might or might not be used. By reproducing this material to assess the 1992 election campaign I do not consider that I have broken any confidences.

CHAPTER 1

WEDNESDAY 11 MARCH

THE BEGINNING – 29 DAYS TO GO

John Major walked through the front door of Number 10 Downing Street at precisely four minues past one. He announced that polling day would be 9 April and his announcement was broadcast live on lunchtime radio and television news. The timing was perfect. Gus O'Donnell, the prime minister's press secretary, had worked in great secrecy to provide the best possible lift off for Mr Major; he knew that once the election was called, control over Mr Major's appearances in the news media would pass from the government's publicity machine to the Conservative party. He was determined to ensure that the Downing Street announcement gained the widest possible news coverage. The statutory notice had been given and parliament would be prorogued and dissolved on Monday 16 March, giving members two days to debate and vote on Mr Lamont's budget.

Reporters had been aware for several days that Mr Major had an audience with the Queen at 6.30 pm on Wednesday 11 March, and there was speculation that the prime minister would seek the dissolution of parliament immediately after the budget, but there was no inkling of the exact timing. Mr O'Donnell's careful planning paid off. Mr Major's announcement dominated the news all day, blotting out the impact of Labour's opposition to the new lower income tax rate of 20 pence in the pound, unveiled by the chancellor,

Norman Lamont.

Nothing was left to chance that morning. Vanessa Ford, a Conservative party press officer, travelled by train to the prime minister's Huntingdon home. When she arrived, at 9 am, Mrs Major whispered to her: 'It's today, you know.' Miss Ford had left London not knowing for sure whether the election would be called that day. 'I rang the press office at Conservative Central Office to tell them. They didn't know either. There were lots of journalists outside ... Mrs Major was very patient as we waited and waited for the announcement.'

Mr O'Donnell arranged for the first official statement to be made at 11 am. An explicit two hour lead time had never been given to journalists before but, in a break with tradition, Downing Street set up a conference telephone call with the leading news agencies to tell them simultaneously that Mr Major would be leaving for Buckingham Palace within the hour. It was essential to prevent this news leaking out in advance. Confirmation that Mr Major was on his way to see the Queen was considered price sensitive information which could affect the stock market. However, Mr O'Donnell's over-riding preoccupation as press secretary was to secure maximum exposure for Mr Major's subsequent appearance on the steps of Number 10. By giving the broadcasting organisations two hours' notice, the press secretary ensured they had ample time to deploy their teams of reporters, camera crews and technicians.

Mr Major has perfected his Downing Street appearances. At the height of the Gulf War and the Soviet coup he often made two or three statements a day, usually broadcast live on radio and television. His preferred technique is to write down the main points on small cards which he checks before emerging from Number 10. By dispensing with a written statement or notes he appears relaxed and he can concentrate on his delivery.

Split-second timing is needed for live coverage, so Mr Major was careful not to walk out to the waiting microphones too soon, otherwise he might either have clashed with the opening titles of the news bulletins or failed to allow sufficient time for programme presenters to hand over to the reporters stationed in Downing Street. Mr O'Donnell takes great pride in arranging orderly doorstep appearances. By holding Mr Major back until exactly four minutes past one he guaranteed the smoothest possible presentation.

The budget, followed by the announcement of polling day, were the last two significant pre-election events over which Mr Major was able to exercise total control. Once a campaign gets under way the government cannot be confident of dictating the news agenda, especially on television and radio. Under a long standing convention, the broadcasting organisations operate a formula for election coverage designed to give equal coverage to the Conservatives and Labour, with a slightly smaller share to the Liberal Democrats.

Mr Major's announcement had an electrifying effect on Labour MPs. At last they saw the promise of a level playing field: the same amount of air time as the Conservatives. In interviews that Wednesday lunchtime, the Labour leader Neil Kinnock sounded elated, buoyed up, he said, by the prospect of equal coverage from the broadcasters.

Also of importance to Labour was the knowledge that strict rules on civil service neutrality are in force throughout an election campaign. These rules are designed to curtail government action favouring the party in power so that, for example, the government's planned advertising campaign on crime prevention was cancelled. But such conventions cut both ways. Relieved of their departmental responsibilities, ministers are free to devote themselves to the campaign. The environment secretary, Michael Heseltine, was impatient to get out on the stump, confident that his electioneering skill would be of great value to Mr Major. A successful campaign would, he believed, help his rehabilitation among those sections of the Conservative party which still resented his action in challenging Mrs Thatcher.

As the election planning intensified Mr Heseltine was selected for the A team, the inner group of cabinet ministers advising Mr Major. They were dubbed the big beasts. Mr Heseltine enjoys his encounters with the news media. Rarely is he thrown by an awkward question and if fed a good line by an interviewer invariably he tries to respond. He was in fine form on Wednesday evening, only too happy to reply to my question about whether he was relishing the prospect of four weeks' campaigning: 'It's as though we have had the leash taken off us.'

DAY 2 THURSDAY 12 MARCH

The long build up to the campaign proved tiresome for politicians and public alike. Despite months of phony electioneering the Conservatives remained neck and neck with Labour in the opinion polls. A general election had to be held by the July deadline, the end of the government's five year term. An April contest always seemed the most likely option after Mr Major decided not to go to the country at the end of the Gulf War or in the autumn of 1991. But by delaying so long, Mr Major and his ministers gave the impression that they were hanging on to power until the last possible moment.

The aim of announcing the election on the morning after the budget was to recapture the votes of skilled workers, or C2s as they are known in marketing jargon, who would benefit by nearly £3 a week from the new lower income tax rate of 20 pence in the pound. Conservative MPs believed the chancellor had effectively ambushed Labour by directing the tax cut to the lower paid. But the pre-budget discussion was dominated by the prime minister's own confirmation that the government was ready to sanction an increase in public borrowing. Labour was already attacking Mr Lamont for seeking to bribe voters with borrowed money. The chancellor's budget admission of a doubling of the borrowing limit to £28 billion added fresh impetus to opposition criticism.

Treasury questions provided some lively exchanges which continued during the final Commons clash between Mr Major and

Mr Kinnock. However, their exchanges concentrated not on the budget but on Mr Kinnock's challenge to the prime minister to join a televised debate.

All three party leaders were approached to take part. The debate was to be organised by the Hansard Society and made available to all television channels. Mr Major refused, saying a debate could be no substitute for the election itself. He had a carefully prepared answer for Mr Kinnock: 'If I accurately recall my Shakespeare: "He draweth out the thread of his verbosity finer than the staple of his argument." Appropriately, that comes from Love's Labour's Lost and Labour will lose.' Mr Kinnock needed little prompting with his supplementary: 'The prime minister reads quotations from Shakespeare. Let me give him one from the right honourable member for Finchley (Mrs Thatcher): "He is frit." '

Labour thought they had Mr Major and his government on the defensive. But the Conservatives had one further tactical advantage. The calling of the election coincided with the annual meeting of the party's central council to be held in Torquay, (it controls all local Conservative Associations). Tory strategists were confident this two day event would provide a springboard for their campaign.

Political conferences are usually well reported by the news media. The organisers place great emphasis on the set piece speeches, hoping they will command most of the attention. But we welcome such gatherings as an opportunity to meet a cross section of party activists. We relish the chance to test out opinion on the key political issues of the day.

The Conservatives were holding their central council meeting in enemy territory. (Central council meetings are held around the country and the venue is booked two to three years in advance. The Conservatives lost control over Torbay Borough Council – to the Liberal Democrats – only ten months before the central council meeting, but a year after Torbay was booked). This reminder of the challenge facing south west Conservative MPs heightened the general air of apprehension.

Michael Dolley, agent for the Torbay Conservatives, told me that he was worried about the strength of the Liberal Democrat advance. He was even prepared to contemplate defeat in this Tory stronghold. The Conservative MP, Rupert Allason, held Torbay with a majority of nearly 8000 in the 1987 election. When I asked Mr Dolley why he feared defeat he said: 'There is a danger we could lose on local issues, such as education. But our one great strength is the chance to exploit the danger of the Liberal Democrats letting Neil Kinnock into Downing Street. There is a large elderly population in the constituency and they will hardly need reminding of the disasters of the Lib–Lab pact of the 1970s and how it led to the winter of discontent.'

Mr Dolley's uncertainty encapsulated the jittery mood of the party officials assembling in Torquay. The Conservatives had failed to open up an opinion poll lead over Labour and they were entering the election without the firm direction of Mrs Thatcher. Tory fortunes rested on the untried campaigning skills of John Major.

DAY 3 FRIDAY 13 MARCH

Torquay's English Riviera Centre resembled a fortress. Officers of the Devon and Cornwall Constabulary were stationed all around the building and most of the entrances were blocked off. Strict security was only to be expected: no police force could afford to relax for a moment after the devastating consequences of the bombing of the Grand Hotel during the Conservatives' 1984 Brighton Conference.

In the months leading up to the election there was speculation about the threat of IRA terrorist action during the campaign. Chris Patten, the Conservative party chairman, had on previous occasions asked journalists for their assessment of the danger. He spoke of his concern about the need to provide adequate insurance cover for young party workers who might be at risk.

Reporters tend to complain all too easily about what we (occasionally) consider time wasting security checks. One such comment produced a swift rebuke from the usually phlegmatic Mr Patten: 'Don't you realise the IRA are trying to kill one of us?' The troubled look on his face emphasised the strain he was under. Mr Patten was having to organise an election campaign when the Conservatives had their backs to the wall while at the same defending his marginal seat in Bath. The problems posed by the need for heightened security precautions obviously added to those pressures.

Unlike some politicians, Mr Patten usually gives every impression of enjoying journalistic banter. At a breakfast briefing for reporters the previous month he happily chatted away about his preference for American expressions like 'gobsmacked.' He seemed particularly proud of his use of 'double whammy' which he said was American for a double punch and was indicative of the double blow on prices and taxes which would be delivered by a Labour government. The erudite Mr Patten thought he had added two useful expressions to election vocabulary. But that breakfast briefing, like the encounter at Torquay, had an unexpected twist. In a revealing reply to a question of mine, prompted by the sight of a set of black and white photographs of his wife Lavender and three daughters, Mr Patten stared at the pictures which were arranged on the wall opposite his desk and then, as if caught in a trance, muttered: 'No, I don't see enough of them.' Mr Patten is usually strict about keeping his family out of politics, rarely having been photographed in public with his daughters.

Mr Patten wore a wistful look as he stood in the car park at the Torquay conference centre waiting to unveil the Conservatives' latest election poster. Four Admobile vans were arranged in a semicircle. Each was covered in a large blue tarpaulin. The assembled newspaper photographers looked bored. Several said the political parties had laid on so many poster unveilings in recent weeks that their pictures were rarely getting used. Mr Patten kept up a stream of one liners in an attempt to keep the press pack amused. 'This isn't a pose. This is natural. You want fists up. Well here's a double whammy for you.' And he raised his fists defiantly.

Amidst all this banality Mr Patten suddenly found himself diverted by a question from *The Independent's* columnist Mark Lawson who inquired why he was using so many Americanisms. Within a matter of seconds the two were locked in animated conversation about the merits of various American authors. A party worker tugged at Mr Patten's sleeve, dragging him back to reality. 'One down and another 18 to go,' said the chairman, looking up again at the poster. It carried the slogan 'You can't trust Labour' and the L was a superimposed red L-plate of the kind used by learner drivers.

The poster had been devised by the Conservatives' advertising agents, Saatchi and Saatchi, and was booked to appear on 5500 billboard sites around the country. Mr Patten promised it would be the biggest poster campaign Britain had ever seen.

However, party strategists have always remained doubtful about the true impact of election advertising. Angie Bray, the chairman's press officer, said that whatever their supposed faults, posters were a useful way of keeping up morale among party supporters. She described how Mr Patten, on leaving the studios of *Channel 4 News* after one particularly gruelling interview, was cheered up by a Tory poster in Gray's Inn Road.

Maurice Saatchi, who was supervising the preparation of the Conservatives' advertising campaign, arrived that morning in the chairman's helicopter, looking windswept with a white silk scarf around his neck. His agency had wisely taken the precaution of placing one of the new L-plate posters on a large billboard site at the point where the A380 reached Torquay. Party representatives arriving by car would be sure to see it on their way to the conference centre.

The chairman's speech lived up to Mark Lawson's expectations. Mr Patten opened with a reworking of President Bush's pledge, which, mythically, had Neil Kinnock saying: 'Read my lips. Lots more taxes.' Then came a rebuke to Labour for having apparently sought the advice of the Manhattan consultants Doak and Schrum on what Mr Patten described as the 'less delicate sort' of campaign tactics.

Michael Heseltine rounded off the afternoon with an onslaught on Labour's planned tax increases, predicting they would be slaughtered at the election. 'Not since the charge of the Light Brigade into the Russian guns at Balaclava will we have seen a slaughter like it. Taxes to the left of them, taxes to the right of them ... into the valley of the taxes rode the Labour party.' He was applauded wildly and congratulated afterwards for steadying the nerves of party workers.

SATURDAY 14 MARCH

John Major's closing speech was to be the highlight of the weekend. His entrance to the conference hall was planned in meticulous detail and was accompanied by the first playing of the Conservatives' new theme music for the campaign. Produced by Andrew Lloyd Webber from theatre music written by Henry Purcell for Abdelazer, the arrangement was described as being 'unpretentious but with deep popular appeal, capturing the spirit of John Major's campaign.' It was arranged in various styles to suit a symphony orchestra or electronic synthesisers.

A stirring, recognisable theme tune has become an essential ingredient when packaging politicians. Political parties hope to establish a sense of expectation among the audience and by playing the theme tune when a leader enters a conference hall, they also hope to influence people watching on television. In order to create the maximum impact the organisers try to make the leader's entrance as dramatic as possible by ensuring that the music reaches its finale at precisely the right moment.

An elaborate dress rehearsal was arranged by Russ Pipe, the Conservatives' director of presentation, to ensure accurate timing for Mr Major's arrival. Increasingly this tends to be done in cooperation with the television crews assigned to cover a speech or conference.

In return for privileged access they are asked to share all film taken between them, or to 'pool' their shots. Unless there is such an agreement, the leader's entrance risks being marred by an unsightly melee as camera crews and photographers jostle for the best positions. Instead, by careful planning, the organisers can take advantage of television's insatiable appetite for fresh pictures. Under a typical pooling arrangement one television crew will be allowed to walk backwards as the speaker proceeds across the conference floor; another will follow from behind. Both crews will be able to get close up shots of the leader's face together with audience reaction. These presidential-style entrances can appear even more dramatic when rounded off by a rousing theme tune.

Another factor which has forcibly improved the relationship between political parties and the news media is the constant need for security. None of the documents for the Torquay conference made any reference to a speech by Mr Major. His name was not mentioned on the diagram showing the route he would take and the only clue was the letters VIP, indicating his likely position on the conference floor and platform.

As the morning progressed the tension increased. Because of bad weather Mr Major could not fly by helicopter to Torquay. Instead he flew to Exeter and was driven on to Torquay. His car swept past the front entrace, pulling up at a rear door.

Inside the conference hall party representatives seemed isolated from the excitement. Mr Major's arrival was signalled first by the lights of the television crews and then the start of the theme tune. The prime minister walked along one aisle and then another, smiling and shaking hands. These long walk-on shots are ideal for television, allowing correspondents to set the scene. Just at the moment the music reached its climax Mr Major leapt up the steps on to the stage. Russ Pipe's timings had proved spot on. As the applause died down Mr Major delivered his opening soundbite: 'Mr chairman, the phony war is over. The Battle of Britain has begun.'

Mr Major used the speech to set out the key issues of the

campaign. Labour's plans for higher taxation revealed a fatal addiction: 'They are high on tax,' declared Mr Major. The campaign for Scottish independence was, in his view, the issue that transcended the election and could lead to the break up of the United Kingdom. Mr Major ridiculed the Liberal Democrats' demand for proportional representation, saying the letters PR stood for 'Paddy's Roundabout.' He assured the conference the Conservatives would not be joining Mr Ashdown for the ride.

Several cabinet colleagues described the speech as the best that Mr Major had delivered. Party workers seemed reassured, confident that their leader could pack the punch required in the weeks that lay ahead. The poster displays showed the Tories had the money and muscle to keep on hitting Labour. But we, in our conversations around the conference hall, detected a strong undercurrent of unease. This uncertainty was evident when party representatives could be persuaded to speculate about the likely result. Many of them revealed a lack of conviction, prefacing their remarks with words like: 'if we win' rather than: 'when we get back.'

SUNDAY 15 MARCH   DAY 5

John Major's speech in Torquay gave the Conservative campaign a kick start, leading Saturday's news bulletins on radio and television. In an attempt to retain that advantage there were plans to present the prime minister in a new election format which the party thought would be ideal for television. Journalists were taken by coach to a village hall in Mr Major's Huntingdon constituency. Surrounded by party members and their friends, Mr Major perched on a stool answering unrehearsed, but definitely friendly, questions. The cosy intimacy was underlined when he stripped off his jacket and continued in his shirt sleeves.

Mr Major modelled his version of a fireside chat on the informal gatherings which he held in the desert with young soldiers when visiting Saudia Arabia during the Gulf War. He seemed well satisfied with his first question and answer session.

The technique of portraying the prime minister as 'Citizen John Major' was regarded as a trump card by the Conservatives' director of communications Shaun Woodward. He was recruited by Chris Patten largely because of his experience as a television producer and editor. Mr Woodward spent eight years with the BBC, working on *Newsnight* and *Panorama* before editing *That's Life*. Mr Woodward staked a great deal on the success of the 'Meet John Major' sessions, believing they would play to the prime minister's strengths. However, there was a danger that the informality of these events would lessen the impact of Mr Major's responses with the result that news bulletins would choose more incisive answers obtained from the tougher questioning of professional interviewers. Mr Major was anxious to have maximum exposure and because of the Conservatives' failure to develop a clear lead in the opinion polls, hurried arrangements were made to bring forward radio and television interviews scheduled for later in the campaign.

While in Torquay, Mr Major was interviewed by Nick Clarke for *Radio Four's The World This Weekend*. The opening questions concentrated on reaction to the budget which was described as a 'damp squib' by the *Sunday Times*. An opinion poll commissioned for the paper showed that 51% of those questioned thought the budget would not improve the Conservatives' chances of winning the election. When this was put to Mr Major he expressed his irritation, saying he was not going to be deflected by such 'silly polls.'

Sunday newspaper criticism of the budget encouraged Labour's treasury team. They had been busy since Tuesday preparing a shadow budget, for the first time ever. Having completed their calculations earlier than expected, Labour were ready for the shadow chancellor, John Smith, to unveil his shadow budget. After a week when the Conservatives held the initiative, Labour insisted they would soon be dictating the news agenda.

CHAPTER 2

MONDAY 16 MARCH DAY **6**

WEEK 2 – 24 DAYS TO GO

Every general election for the last half century has been accompanied by an expansion in what politicians dismiss as the media circus. The ending of wartime restrictions on the use of newsprint, followed in more recent years by the hectic growth of radio and television, has necessitated constant adjustment by the political parties as they seek to find ways of exploiting the fresh opportunities presented by the continued diversification of the news media.

Like its predecessors, the 1992 election held out the prospect of even more media coverage. The launch of satellite television enabled *Sky News* to offer 24 hour news coverage. BBC *Radio Four* allocated an extra 30 hours broadcasting a week to its election coverage, becoming almost a rolling news service at some points in the day.

The power of television and radio to dominate the reporting of elections became firmly entrenched in the early 1980s. The rapid spread of local radio stations was followed by the introduction of breakfast television. By the 1983 election the political parties could plan their campaigns to take advantage of television and radio news outlets which would be operating morning, noon and night. The opportunity to participate in a non-stop national and local arena of news bulletins and discussion programmes was there for the taking.

Perhaps there is no better illustration of the contradiction in the love–hate relationship between politicians and the news media than the politicians' determination to achieve the largest possible share of this expanded news coverage. Each party attempts to get in first and, at the same time, to do whatever is possible to sabotage the publicity initiatives of their opponents.

In the weeks leading up to the election, as the three parties planned their campaign tactics, there was considerable jockeying for the prize news slot each morning. Because the Conservatives opted to hold their daily news conference at 8.30 am, Labour went for 7.45 am and the Liberal Democrats, anxious not to end up tail-end Charlie, plumped for 7.15 am. This was a calculated attempt by the parties to try to cash in on the increased audiences for breakfast television.

Journalists greeted the prospect of such an early start to daily news conferences with trepidation. Newspaper reporters complained most of all, blaming politicians for being infatuated with television. However, the parties relented on this, the first Monday of the cam-paign, preferring a later start as they had weighty matters to promote.

First stop was the National Liberal Club where the library had been converted into a small, intimate theatre with tiered rows of seats. Journalists looked down on the platform. Alongside Paddy Ashdown were his campaign director Des Wilson and the Liberal Democrats treasury spokesman Alan Beith. The set, which was used throughout the campaign, looked clinically white except for a yellow strip. Television monitors on the wall beamed pictures of the Liberal Democrats orange campaign badge bearing the slogan 'My vote.'

Five rows up from the front of the platform sat Mr Ashdown's wife Jane, wearing a blue jumper and a turquoise skirt. She looked pensive, holding her index finger to her chin, as Mr Ashdown welcomed reporters to the launch of his party's manifesto. The Liberal Democrats were obviously delighted to be first off the mark. Their manifesto was certainly distinctive, and nearly twice the size of most similar publications; presumably in the hope it would stand out when displayed on bookstalls.

Mr Ashdown was ready with a dramatic opening line: 'Be

warned, this manifesto might not be what you expect.' His ringing declaration suited the theatrical surroundings. He said the Liberal Democrats were determined to tell the truth about how Britain had been dragged down by 40 years of failed government and an out of date electoral system.

Later, when Des Wilson was answering questions about their campaign strategy, Mr Ashdown glanced up. Straining against the glare of the television lights, he looked for his wife. They both sneaked a smile. Mr Ashdown seemed pleased the manifesto launch had gone so well. Only five weeks had elapsed since his dramatic statement disclosing details of a brief personal relationship with a former secretary.

As the news conference broke up Mrs Ashdown watched from her seat as the party's senior media officer Olly Grender whisked her husband away for a round of television interviews. Finally, the questions over, Mr Ashdown walked back onto the platform. He seemed rather fretful, looking intently at the shiny steel framework which had been erected in front of the backing to the platform. 'This contraption is supposed to make our set look modern and urgent. What do you think? Does it look cluttered? I won't know for sure until I see what it looks like on television.'

Every Liberal Democrat has to be ready to be a jack of all trades, so limited are the party's resources. Mr Ashdown is no exception, appearing to enjoy any opportunity to get immersed in the tiniest detail of presentation, sometimes to the despair of his staff. The Liberal Democrats could not have had a more willing and able graduate from the tough media assault course which awaits newly-appointed political leaders. The loyalty which Mr Ashdown is reputed to have inspired in his days as a marine commando has been repeated at Westminster: we rated him as the most user-friendly of the three party leaders.

Mr Ashdown's hopes that the publication of his party's manifesto might dominate the news that day were not fulfilled. Labour's treasury team, having completed the calculations for their shadow budget earlier than expected, were intent on upstaging the Liberal Democrats. The shadow chancellor, John Smith, and his five colleagues organised a cheeky photo-opportunity. They stood together, posing for the cameras on the steps of the treasury, holding up copies of Labour's answer to Norman Lamont's budget.

Mr Smith and his team had invested a great deal of effort preparing their alternative tax and benefits package which, it was predicted, would result in eight out of ten families being better off. By judiciously leaking some of the details in advance to a few trusted reporters, Labour had already created quite a stir in the news media. After the less than ecstatic reception for Mr Lamont's budget, Neil Kinnock saw this as an opportunity to present Labour as the government in waiting.

An air of excited anticipation greeted journalists as we assembled in the oak panelled lecture room of the Institution of Civil Engineers. On this occasion, unlike a normal news conference, no press releases were handed out as we arrived. We were told that a red book, similar to the one produced by the treasury, would be released as soon as Mr Smith completed his statement. Labour seemed intent on trying to reproduce the traditional budget speech.

Mr Kinnock led his treasury team on to the platform. He smiled, only too ready to wait a few moments as the camera crews and photographers jostled for the best positions. This was a moment to savour. The shadow chancellor was about to outline a package of proposals which the Labour leadership was convinced would outbid the Conservatives and perhaps clinch the election for Labour.

Mr Smith began with an assessment of Britain's economic prospects and then launched into his detailed proposals. The central plank of the shadow budget was a promise to increase personal allowances and, as a result, take 740 000 people out of income tax altogether. Once the proposed increase in child benefit was included, Labour estimated that the average two earner family with two children would see its disposable income rise by £311 a year.

The moment John Smith finished speaking, press officers handed round copies of Labour's red book listing the various calculations. When the shadow chancellor was challenged about the impact of Labour's higher tax and national insurance on those with incomes of above £22 000, Mr Smith said that the Conservatives had spent 13 years ensuring people at the top did better, now Labour were speaking up for the average taxpayer. His firm response, as with earlier answers, was greeted with applause from Labour researchers and party activists who crowded into the lecture room.

The applause disconcerted me and a number of reporters. Several said later that they found the applause intimidating. We were reluctant to participate because if Mr Smith's answers to our questions were applauded, that applause might be interpreted as an endorsement of his answers and, if seen on television, could detract from our impartiality as journalists. One of the party workers clapping at the front of the room, rather like a cheer leader, was Julie Hall, Mr Kinnock's press secretary. She was a political correspondent for ITN before being recruited to the Labour leader's private office in 1989.

Whatever else might have been intended, the applause underlined the effectiveness of Labour's stage management. We were impressed by the authoritative nature of Mr Smith's presentation. The Conservatives had arranged a rival attraction to coincide with the shadow budget, in an attempt to divert the news media's attention. Drawn up outside party headquarters in Smith Square was the campaign coach to be used by the prime minister.

On taking delivery, Mr Major described it as 'fabulous.' The coach was designed as a mobile communications centre, complete with computer terminals, cellular telephones and fax machines. The in-built security precautions were awesome: two tons of armour plating and bullet-proof glass. While Mr Major entertained the media, Mr Lamont and four other cabinet ministers were hard at work inside Central Office analysing Labour's shadow budget.

A hurried news conference was arranged so that the chancellor could respond to Mr Smith's proposals. It started 15 minutes later

25

than planned and as we waited there was a flurry of excitement. In what seemed a rather blatant attempt to upstage Mr Lamont, copies of an assessment by the Institute of Fiscal Studies were being handed round surreptitiously. The document suggested that 80% of people would be better off under Labour while only 74% would gain from the Conservatives' budget. Mr Lamont considered the shadow budget would have three immediate consequences: interest rates would rise; house prices would be devastated; and taxes would soar.

Within two-and-a-half-hours of Mr Smith's speech, the Conservatives claimed to have shredded Labour's proposals. Chris Patten thought the chancellor's counter offensive was highly successful, concluding that the shadow budget only compounded Labour's original error in proposing tax increases. Nevertheless, there were no such qualms that evening at a joint meeting of the shadow cabinet and Labour's national executive committee which, in giving final approval to the party's manifesto, regarded Mr Smith's statement as the cornerstone of Labour's campaign.

Journalists and television crews waited outside in the knowledge that this was the last occasion when we might witness internal opposition. The meeting was much shorter than in previous elections, having been conducted, said the party chairman John Evans, in 'very good humour.' Several issues were pressed to a vote but they were each heavily defeated. Mr Evans assured reporters there was no serious dissent. Tony Benn and Dennis Skinner, the two left wing executive members who regularly challenge the leadership, both hurried away refusing to be interviewed. Mr Skinner shouted back to us: 'What do you expect? I am a candidate.'

Throughout the run up to the election there was little or no public criticism of the party leadership, either from the left of the parliamentary party or from trade union leaders who were known to dislike Mr Kinnock. This lack of criticism had unnerved Tory party strategists who had been hoping to exploit divisions within the Labour party. The silence was a calculated move: leading figures on the left had agreed the previous year there would be no public dissent during the election so that they could not be blamed in the event of Mr Kinnock being defeated.

TUESDAY 17 MARCH   DAY 7

One consequence of holding the election on 9 April was that the first week of the campaign would automatically coincide with a run of potentially unfavourable economic statistics, including figures for industrial production, unemployment and inflation. The Conservatives were anxious to deflect attention from the sharper than expected fall in manufacturing output, and decided to field Mr Major at the first of what he promised would be daily news conferences. He pre-empted the launch of his own manifesto by unveiling the party's plans on education, billed as 'Thirty-nine Steps to Higher Standards.' Later, Mr Kinnock described the document as representing thirty-nine steps backwards.

All three parties tried to maintain an element of surprise about the topic to be discussed at their news conferences each morning. A vague hint would be given the night before but details of any policy initiatives remained shrouded in secrecy so as to give their opponents as little time as possible to react. Labour's director of communications, David Hill, assigned a team of press officers to prepare a wide range of news stories and photo-opportunities for last minute use in the hope of frustrating the Conservatives. Once it was discovered early on Tuesday morning that the Tories had chosen to go on education, Labour announced they would hold a rival news conference early in the afternoon.

A former BBC producer, Phil Woolas, devised Labour's counter attraction. The mother of a six-year-old south London schoolboy, Fraser Duckworth, had agreed to keep her son on standby during the campaign. After a telephone call in the morning the boy's mother obtained approval from Fraser's head teacher to take him off school for the afternoon. She waited with her son in the front row of Labour's news conference until he was called up by Labour's campaign director Jack Cunningham. Fraser was told to sit on a chair which had been placed in full view of the television cameras. On his lap were placed copies of the 165 educational changes which were introduced during 13 years of Conservative government. Slowly Fraser's face disappeared behind a three foot pile of documents. At that point Labour's education spokesman Jack Straw explained that school standards had declined because headmasters were submerged beneath a flood of ill-digested policy changes.

Fraser's photo-opportunity was featured extensively in the evening television news bulletins, providing a graphic illustration of Labour's claim that schools were already overburdened with change. Mr Woolas was pleased with the impact he achieved. He devised several similar television sequences aimed at undermining the Conservatives' campaign.

There is always a danger that stunts of this kind will appear unnatural and contrived, but Mr Woolas said that his experience as a producer on *Newsnight* and *Channel 4 News* had enabled him to think up 'look aheads' as they are called, which had a strong news line and an air of spontaneity. Mr Woolas left journalism the previous year to become head of communications for the General Municipal and Boilermakers Union (GMB), and he was one of several union press officers seconded to assist behind the scenes with Labour's campaign.

Mr Major matched messages with pictures, posing with children at a primary school near the RAF base at Waddington in Lincolnshire. All three party leaders were on the campaign trail. Mr Major flew to Waddington in a BAe 146 hired for the campaign; Mr Kinnock travelled by train to Bristol in the 'Red Rose Express,' a 125 Intercity chartered from British Rail; and Mr Ashdown tried out his canary yellow campaign coach on a tour of London constituencies.

But despite their best efforts to set the news agenda, all three parties found that the opinion polls had captured the headlines that day. That evening news emerged of opinion polls to be published the following day in *The Times* and *The Guardian* which both suggested that Labour had a five-point lead over the Conservatives.

Journalists following Mr Major's campaign were alerted by their newsrooms and asked to get his reaction. However, on the flight back to London the prime minister remained in the section of the plane screened off for his private use. Mr Major seemed edgy when questioned earlier about the figures for industrial output. At one point he refused to take any further questions on the recession, placing his hand over a radio correspondent's microphone. The incident was insignificant, no more than the usual cut and thrust of an election walkabout, but it illustrates the tension that can develop.

WEDNESDAY 18 MARCH DAY 8

Labour could hardly have expected a more propitious backdrop for the launch of their manifesto. Identical front page headlines appeared in *The Times* and *The Guardian*: 'Labour takes a five point lead.' The *Daily Telegraph's* lead story had the headline: 'Polls predict nine seat win for Labour.' The two parties arranged to publish their manifestos within an hour-and-a-half of each other but Labour, opting to go first, put the Conservatives on the defensive.

Labour arranged for their manifesto launch to take place at the party's temporary media centre at 4 Millbank, a refurbished office block which contains the Westminster studios of the main broadcasting organisations. Taking space at Millbank for news conferences and briefings is an astute move because it ensures easy access for television and radio journalists.

Rather unwisely Labour apparently omitted to carry out an adequate test of security procedures. Journalists queued to reach the conference room and the start of the proceedings was delayed. So great was the crush that the campaign theme music *Time for*

Change, composed by Michael Kamen, finished before Neil Kinnock and the shadow cabinet reached the platform. David Blunkett, who was sitting among the reporters with his guide dog Offa, smiled on hearing the explanation for the journalists' laughter. He was listening intently to the tune and whispered to me: 'I think the music signals prudence rather than radicalism.' On Mr Blunkett's lap was a braille copy of the manifesto.

Mr Kinnock introduced the manifesto, entitled 'It's Time to Get Britain Working Again,' by saying it contained the down-to-earth policies needed for a country hit by recession. Most of the questions concerned Labour's plans for British Telecom, British Gas and other privatised industries such as water. When one reporter asked Mr Kinnock if he would resign if he lost the election, there were noisy protests from members of the shadow cabinet lined up on the platform. Mr Kinnock seemed amused by the strength of their rebuttal: 'That was what you could describe as a collectively derisive response . . . We are not going to lose the election. We are going to win, and we will be the government.'

The Conservatives hired the Queen Elizabeth II conference centre across the road from Westminster Abbey for the launch of their manifesto. On either side of the platform were two enormous pictures of John Major together with the slogan 'The Best Future for Britain': the title of the manifesto. The cabinet filed in first. Norman Lamont's face was pale and drawn, contrasting starkly with Michael Heseltine's ruddy cheeks. Mr Major was applauded as he walked on to the platform with Chris Patten. Norma Major sat on one of the press seats. I overheard party workers anxiously saying that they must make sure journalists did not get too close to Mrs Major because we might ask awkward questions and she might find this unsettling.

Next to Mrs Major sat Sir Basil Feldman, chairman of the Conservatives' executive committee, and immediately in front was her press officer Vanessa Ford. Mr Major stated the aim of the manifesto: to open the door to a new Britain through which 'more people ... many more people ... can find their way to the warmth and light of achievement and ownership.' When a journalist suggested that the manifesto was Mrs Thatcher's with Mr Major's name on it, the prime minister retorted: 'It's all Major. Every last word of it is me. Every single bit of it. What's set out in here is the sort of Britain I want to see, the sort of Britain I will lead this country towards.'

We laughed at this spirited answer but the uplift was short-lived. Behind the confident facade there was a high degree of tension. Immediately the news conference finished ministers were busy pressing the flesh, telling journalists not to believe the suggestions that Labour's campaign was proving more effective. However, rather surprisingly, two former Tory party chairmen were only too ready to give their advice on tactics.

The home secretary, Kenneth Baker, told me that the Conservatives needed to put some 'flint and fire' into their campaign, and Norman Tebbit thought the Tories should go for Labour's jugular. It was time, said Mr Tebbit, to bring on 'the dogs of war.' Armed with these quotes I searched out the Conservatives' director of communications Shaun Woodward. 'Was there going to be a crisis meeting,' I asked, 'to consider what had gone wrong with the campaign?' Mr Woodward was not going to be caught out so easily, and instead, realising that attack was the best form of defence, launched into a tirade of criticism against his opponents.

'Look what happened yesterday,' said Mr Woodward. 'Kinnock caught a train, ate some breakfast and then arrived in Bristol. He walked round a railway station protected by his minders, was filmed shaking hands and then went to a school. Is that supposed to be a high-key campaign? Compare that with John Major in front of an audience of 300, taking awkward questions. That is Major opening himself up to people. That is high-wire campaigning. These meet the people sessions really are Majorcentric. They are producing tremendous pictures in the newspapers and on television.'

Mr Woodward insisted he was not being defensive. He said 3000 more posters were due to go up at 4 pm and the party's first election broadcast would be that evening. 'Our broadcast is all about Major. It is not one of those Kinnock party politicals that leaves you feeling as if you have seen *Chariots of Fire*. Major talks about the issues. Major is real. In our broadcast Major talks about his life in Brixton and then says why he is not a socialist. That is compelling.'

After the manifesto launch, Mr Major faced a series of television interviews which provided an unexpected, but telling, counterpoint to some of Mr Woodward's assertions about the strength of the prime minister's performance. Most politicians are extremely wary of television and radio studios, sensing danger the moment they get within range of a camera or a microphone. They tend to avoid off-the-cuff remarks, on the assumption that an interview has started the moment they walk through the studio door. Politicians have learned to their cost the damage that can be inflicted if just one word is broadcast or printed out of context. Mrs Thatcher's reputation was legendary: the only small talk she allowed herself was to enquire about the origin of the liquid in the glass on the studio table. Her insistence on British rather than French bottled water was duly noted.

By contrast Mr Major had few inhibitions. He readily engaged in conversation, apparently unconcerned that his warm-up remarks might be more revealing than the interview itself. This was all the more surprising because on becoming prime minister he started taking a close interest in the way he was presented on television. He is known to be an assiduous channel hopper at news time, especially in the early evening when broadcasters give their first assessment of the day's political news.

Mr Major's total recall is impressive: Downing Street advisers say that he can reel off his placing in each of the news bulletins. If he is concerned about a particular broadcast and wishes to make an immediate complaint, his detailed knowledge can be used to good effect by his press office. The precision of such complaints gets to the heart of news judgment: journalists find themselves being put on the spot, having to justify their very phraseology or choice of interviewees.

Mr Major's preoccupation with his television image surfaced during a preliminary chat before he was questioned on the manifesto. While waiting for the recording to start Mr Major enquired why he always appeared in long shot whereas Mr Kinnock was filmed in close up. 'This has happened for the last three days. Long shots are not as good. I look rather lonely. I much prefer close ups, I think, for the reason of intimacy. If you look as though you are a long way away you appear to be haranguing people, not talking to them. Perhaps it is just the preference of the cameramen. I am not suggesting a plot.' Mr Major sensed that his remarks might imply insecurity on his part and he quickly turned the conversation into a joke, suggesting the explanation was probably due to the fact that Mr Kinnock was better looking. In a break between interviews Mr Major asked what he looked like. 'Is make up OK? I don't look like Yorick, do I?' His persistent but easy-going manner reflected his readiness to dive in when confronted by reporters.

Because of the speed with which he was propelled into the premiership, Mr Major was not bloodied first by the news media. At no point in his short ministerial career was he subjected to the kind of hatred and vilification heaped upon the head of his predecessor when, in 1971 as education secretary, she withdrew free school milk and was dubbed 'Thatcher, Thatcher, Milk Snatcher.' That incident ended any attempt by Mrs Thatcher to establish a working relationship with any section of the media. But Mr Major displayed no such hang-ups. Instead he impressed us with his interest in our opinions and his seemingly inexhaustable supply of friendly conversation.

Inevitably Mr Major's relationship with the media cropped up during interviews. Reporters wanted to know whether he was affected by the campaign. Labour sought to suggest that Mr Major would not withstand the pressures of a tough election. Their claim was given a degree of credence by a former Conservative party director of communications, Brendan Bruce, who was appearing regularly on television and radio programmes giving an insider's view on the competence of the image makers. Mr Bruce expressed concern at a slide in Mr Major's personal popularity rating, and feared this could be damaging to the Tory party campaign because the prime minister was their greatest asset. He warned that Mr Major might find himself in difficulty if needled by interviewers because of his known sensitivity to criticism. Mr Major met the point head on, insisting politicians got used to it. 'I could not honestly claim to like criticism. People think all politicians have a second hide as tough as an armadillo. Not true. But I can be very detached. I can push criticism to one side without it personally disturbing me. I can do that more easily than many people suppose.'

Encouraged by the opinion polls, Mr Kinnock had set off in a jaunty mood for his interviews on Labour's manifesto. At one point, when asked to say a few words so that a sound recordist could check the level of his voice, Mr Kinnock started singing in Welsh. Both leaders are proud of their roots. In the 1987 general election one highlight of Labour's campaign was the election broadcast directed by Hugh Hudson which was dubbed 'Kinnock: The Movie,' depicting Neil and Glenys walking along a cliff top to the strains of Brahms. Labour were flattered when the Conservatives commissioned John Schlesinger to direct a similar movie 'John Major: The Journey.'

Mr Major provided his own commentary for the trip back to his old haunts. He was shown being driven through the streets of Brixton, pointing out the different houses where he spent his youth. A short walk-about round Brixton Market produced a poignant recollection: 'When I was in my early teens, I used occasionally to erect a soapbox and I had two soapboxes, one that I erected in Brixton Market and the other in Brixton Road. I used to talk about political matters of the day and everyone was very tolerant. Some people used to listen, some used to engage in badinage, lots of other people smiled cheerfully and moved on . . . but it was very good experience.'

An announcement from Buckingham Palace that the Duke and Duchess of York were to separate after a six year marriage pushed the publication of the monthly unemployment figures well down the news agenda. These statistics were the ones the Conservatives feared most in a week when they were dogged by uncomfortable reminders of the recession. News of the royal separation broke the day before and there was an audible sigh of relief at Central Office when election coverage took second place.

Unemployment had risen by more than 36 000, taking the total to well over 2.7 million. Of even greater embarrassment to the government was the fact that the February unemployment figure marked an awkward landmark: the cumulative increase in seasonally adjusted unemployment had passed 1 million for the first time since the jobless total started rising in April 1990.

At a poorly attended news conference, where the Conservatives unveiled a new poster suggesting strikes would increase under Labour, the employment secretary Michael Howard was pressed repeatedly by us to admit that the February unemployment figure confirmed that unemployment was rising inexorably. Mr Howard demonstrated his firm grasp of the statistics: 'The three month trend shows a slight increase. The six month trend shows a fall. If you look at this month's figure, it is less than last month's figure, and less than half of what the figure was a year ago.'

Outside in Smith Square, as Mr Howard unveiled the new poster bearing the slogan 'Labour In, Everybody Out' a lone protester shouted: 'That's a load of old rubbish. What about the unemployment figures then?' Mr Howard told the heckler it would not help the unemployed to have more strikes. The employment secretary seemed rather bruised by our aggressive questioning.

The start of the election campaign saw a marked shift in the tone adopted by politicians when responding to reporters' questions. The party leaders realised the value of flattery. Mr Kinnock, despite having little patience with many journalists, behaved impeccably at his televised news conferences, answering on first name terms even if the questioner worked for a Conservative-leaning newspaper. Mr Major had made it his regular habit, since perfecting his doorstep appearances in Downing Street, to include the first name of television reporters in every answer. He found that these personalised responses had the best chance of becoming the soundbites used by the broadcasters.

After the publicity attracted by Mr Major for the election broadcast on his early years in Brixton, journalists were invited to a preview of Hugh Hudson's latest production for Labour. Jack Cunningham described it as a 'blockbuster.' He predicted that the new broadcast, like the 1987 'Kinnock: The Movie,' would set a standard that other parties would try to emulate. The opening pictures were of mountains, woods and lakes with a voice-over from Mr Kinnock, followed by short statements from senior members of the shadow cabinet.

Most journalistic attention focussed on what seemed to be a blurring of portfolios. Only six members of the shadow cabinet were featured, yet they dealt with the whole range of Labour policy. Notable absentees from the broadcast were the shadow foreign secretary Gerald Kaufman, transport spokesman John Prescott and social security spokesman Michael Meacher. I knew from my own discussions with members of the shadow cabinet that the promotion of only a handful of them – those who were deemed telegenic – had caused deep resentment within the shadow cabinet.

Nevertheless, there was a degree of surprise at the transformation which Mr Hudson achieved in the demeanour of the trade and industry spokesman, Gordon Brown, who was filmed smiling and relaxed. In his regular television interviews on the recession Mr Brown always made a point of appearing serious, reflecting his concern not to make light of the problems faced by the bankrupt and the unemployed. However, his downcast delivery became the butt of parliamentary crossfire and he was christened 'Mr Glum' by the trade and industry secretary, Peter Lilley, who thought Mr Brown was in danger of overdosing on gloom.

The sight of Mr Brown looking cheerful provoked an immediate response from Elinor Goodman, political editor of *Channel 4 News*. 'I have never seen Gordon smile before. Doesn't he look natural?' Mr Brown confided to me later that his mother had been telling him for years that it was time he started smiling on television.

The most significant event of the day for the Conservatives occurred during a walk about in Bolton when Mr and Mrs Major were jostled by demonstrators. A ring of police officers struggled desperately to keep the protestors away but the prime minister was swept along by the pressure of the crowd. Labour were accused of sending along a rent-a-mob but the charge was vehemently denied.

Party officials said Mr Major was incensed by the demonstration and the fact that it prevented him from talking to local supporters. The incident seemed to fire him up. At his first campaign rally that evening he surprised journalists with a vitriolic attack on Labour's plans for higher tax and national insurance, describing them as 'a devil's cocktail of incompetence and malice.' Mr Major made great play of the impact he thought this 'fast-spreading cancer' would have on middle income families. He listed traditional Tory supporters like shopkeepers, builders and tradespeople whose livelihoods would be blighted.

Mr Major's speech was delivered from a custom-built arena, complete with huge video screens erected inside a hangar at Manchester airport. Andrew Lloyd Webber reportedly spent £500 000 creating the 'John Major Roadshow,' hoping that it would be as spectacular as one of his own West End shows. The Conservatives' star turn had advance bookings lined up for the next three weeks but the promoters remained uneasy. Audience reaction was proving difficult to assess.

CHAPTER 3

Nothing illustrated more clearly the wretchedness of cabinet ministers in the opening days of the campaign than their discomfort at the government's failure to deliver a pre-election fall in the rate of inflation. Political correspondents could not be dissuaded from talking up the prospect of a small reduction in the monthly rate. However, on the evening before publication, attempts to gauge the confidence of ministers proved unrewarding. Both the employment secretary, Michael Howard, and the trade and industry secretary, Peter Lilley, were distinctly edgy when approached.

The Central Statistical Office (CSO), gives ministers 24 hours' advance warning each month of the headline inflation figure, before the formal announcement is made at 11.30 am on a Friday morning. News agency reporters assemble at 11 am inside CSO headquarters and officials give an unattributable briefing on the monthly figure. At 11.28 am we are told we can make establishing calls to our newsrooms. (An establishing call allows us to keep the line open but not to divulge any information). When a bell rings at 11.30 am we are allowed to release the inflation figure. Great secrecy is insisted upon because inflation statistics are market sensitive. However, on this particular day, some journalists already knew the figure: they had been tipped off the night before by contacts in Whitehall.

Prices rose by 4.1% in the year to February, unchanged from the previous month, despite ministers' hopes that the rate might have fallen to 4%. John Major denied there had ever been any expectation of a reduction. He described the figure as remarkable. For the first time for a quarter of a century Britain's inflation rate was lower than that of Germany.

Earlier, at his morning news conference, Mr Major attacked Labour over the demonstration which had taken place in Bolton the previous afternoon, claiming it had changed the tone of the election. 'What we saw yesterday was the ugly, intolerant face of the Labour party, a mob, obscene gestures, ugly chants, the return of the flying picket.' Neil Kinnock said he knew nothing of the incident and thought the prime minister's protests only indicated the paucity of his thinking. Labour believed Mr Major's outburst smacked of desperation at a time when he was facing increasing criticism from within his party for a lacklustre campaign.

All week there were signs of discontent in the Tory press but there was nothing to equal a trenchant article by Charles Moore which appeared in the *Daily Telegraph*. He described the Conservative campaign as a disgrace, accusing cabinet ministers of burbling. 'They look like men who are so worried about their jobs that they cannot talk clearly to the people in whose hands those jobs lie ... the voters of Britain.'

Mr Moore's criticism added to the tension at Central Office where journalists found the unfavourable publicity creating a backlash against the news media. A request by Joy Johnson, the BBC's political news organiser at Westminster, for increased access for television crews was refused by the director of communications, Shaun Woodward. He was adamant. 'Why should I grant you behind the scenes facilities? Even if I did, I expect the BBC would only say it was tame.' Use of the word 'tame' signified the reason for Mr Woodward's anger. The previous Sunday, in his report on the first of the 'Meet John Major' sessions, John Simpson, the BBC's foreign editor, described the occasion as being 'desperately tame.'

This unflattering review mortified Mr Woodward whose plans to present Mr Major at intimate gatherings, where questions could be answered informally, had already attracted internal criticism. A succession of rapid changes in the party's press and publicity departments resulted in disaffection, especially among long serving staff, some of whom apparently took great delight telling Mr Woodward that Mrs Thatcher would never have allowed herself to be talked into sitting on a bar stool in the middle of a village hall. Mr Woodward felt attacked by us and by senior colleagues in his own party's press and publicity departments.

Mr Woodward was also angered by the *Today* newspaper. Its columnist David Seymour described the director of communications and his team as 'Patten's puppies,' bemoaning the fact that the fate of Mr Major rested in 'a few clammy palms.' Mr Seymour heaped abuse on the Conservatives for having allowed Mr Woodward, who is in his early thirties, to recruit a 'young motley crew' of assistants in their mid and early twenties.

The nub of *Today*'s criticism was that Mr Woodward's team failed utterly to stimulate the Conservative campaign and the likely consequence was that Mr Major would lose the election due to 'rotten organisation and ineffective publicity.' Paul Wilenius, *Today*'s political editor, remarked ruefully: 'Yes, they are a little shirty with us this morning over at Central Office.'

Some cabinet ministers were prepared to acknowledge privately that mistakes had been made. David Mellor, the treasury chief secretary, told me that he was concerned that the Conservatives could lose sight of 'the jewels in a not very outstanding collection.' Central Office's researchers had been calculating the cost of Labour's spending plans – without the help of the treasury because of the rules governing civil service neutrality during an election campaign – and David Mellor thought that the new calculations would shock people. 'Obviously the voters who made it a walk-over for us in 1987 are stroking their chins and thinking it over. If Labour had come up with a big idea it would all be over by now, but they haven't, and that is why the differences between us on tax and public spending are so vital to our campaign.'

Mr Mellor's underlying confidence was in marked contrast to the Friday afternoon gloom which descended in the Westminster offices of political correspondents on Conservative-supporting newspapers. Heaps of Tory press releases, delivered to the House of Commons by the Central Office messenger, Sam Anderson, lay undisturbed on the reception desk in the press gallery. It seemed to me that some of the political correspondents on the Conservative-leaning newspapers were losing heart.

A *Daily Mail* journalist looked dejected, saying they could not go on just 'reheating all those loony Labour stories.' There seemed genuine anger over the apparent failure of the Conservative campaign. 'When are Patten's puppies going to get their act together? Don't they realise that under Labour and their tax plans, the whole of the south east will become suicide valley?' This sense of foreboding was reinforced by a poll published earlier in the afternoon which gave Labour a three point lead in London marginal constituencies.

In his speech that evening Mr Major linked the demonstration in Bolton with Labour's tax plans. Hard style socialism was now bubbling to the surface with 'rent-a-mob in Bolton market and mug the middle incomes on the treasury steps.' But Labour remained unperturbed, busily stoking up reports of panic in the Tory camp. They were assisted in this by London Weekend Television's (LWT) confirmation that Mr Major had brought forward his interview on the *Walden* programme. This was originally scheduled for the last Sunday of the campaign. LWT said: 'We thought the prime minister would have preferred the last word, but his office has told us he can only manage this weekend. We are very grateful to Paddy Ashdown for agreeing to postpone his interview which was originally scheduled for this Sunday.'

LWT's statement was seized on with delight by Labour's director of communications, David Hill. He claimed the *Walden* interview had been brought forward because the Conservatives obviously thought they were going to lose. 'Major is their only asset. They have nowhere else to turn. Even the broadcasters are starting to say that the Conservatives' campaign is entirely negative.'

Mr Hill was assiduous in his efforts to keep in contact with the rota of duty correspondents on television and radio. He had been Labour's director of communications for less than a year but he was well known at Westminster having been Roy Hattersley's political adviser for almost 20 years. Mr Hill considered himself an old hand at briefing political journalists. Unlike his counterparts at Central Office he seemed to have a greater appreciation of the complexities of 24 hour news operations. He realised that if his staff could keep pace with the confusing, but inevitable, rotation of correspondents then Labour could maintain superior lines of communication with the broadcasting organisations and news agencies.

His assessment of the second week was particularly upbeat. Mr Hill thought Labour were successfully presenting Mr Kinnock as remaining above the fray. 'Major is already looking like a man out on the stump, trying to win votes. He is looking like a leader of the opposition and Neil is coming over as the prime minister. The Tories are running hard to catch up.'

DAY 11   SATURDAY 21 MARCH

The Conservatives succeeded in recosting Labour's entire spending programme. Research staff worked until 1 am updating their previous calculations and assessing the likely cost of each pledge in the Labour manifesto. Political correspondents were invited to a news conference to be chaired by John Major. By briefing the news media on Saturday morning the Conservatives hoped their latest estimate of Labour's spending plans would make an impact in the Sunday newspapers and help the Conservatives regain the initiative.

Journalists arriving for the news conference found Smith Square cordoned off by police because of a security alert. Positive readings were recorded on two machines used in Tory party headquarters to check for explosive substances. A Danish reporter, Stine Leth-Nissen of *Det Fri Alktuelt*, arrived early and was standing in the reception area. 'Suddenly your prime minister came down the stairs and walked straight past me out into the square. He led the way with other people behind him. I could not understand what was happening. Then, some minutes later, we were all told to leave because of a security alert.'

Mr Major took refuge nearby in Lord North Street at the home of Conservative MP Alistair Goodlad. He was joined there by Norman Lamont and senior party workers. When it became clear that the security sweep in Central Office would take some time to complete, Mr Major's car drew up and he returned to Downing Street. There was no government car for Mr Lamont who pushed his way through the waiting journalists and walked off rather forlornly down Great Peter Street.

We were told that the news conference would be rescheduled for later in the morning and so we departed for a Labour briefing on the plan for a national minimum wage. Labour's communications team were surprised when we arrived without any indication of what the Conservatives intended revealing. David Hill assumed that Shaun Woodward would at least have distributed press releases to provoke the Labour camp and try to upstage Labour's news conference. Mr Woodward must have realised valuable time had been lost because at 11.07 am the Press Association news agency reported that the Conservatives had costed Labour's spending plans at £38 billion, estimating this would cost the average taxpayer £1250 a year.

Staff were allowed to return to Central Office after it was found that fumes from a computer had triggered the security alert. Mr Major welcomed us back to the delayed briefing, handing over to Mr Lamont, who explained that their previous estimate of £37 billion for the cost of Labour's spending commitments had now been revised upwards by £1 billion following publication of Labour's manifesto.

David Mellor stood beside the chancellor pulling down posters revealing each new costing. The treasury chief secretary looked delighted with his role, which appeared to resemble that of a smiling hostess in the television game show *Double Your Money*. After insisting that the £38 billion estimate was 'a genuine, objective analysis' and not 'taken out of a hat' Mr Mellor revealed his own calculation. There were 12 735 words in Labour's manifesto and as each word would cost the taxpayer £3 million, he thought this worthy of a place in the Guinness Book of Records.

On arriving at the news conference we were each handed a sealed envelope marked 'Tax demand.' Inside was a list of examples for different salary levels, quoting £2365 as the extra tax on an income of £25 000. On completion of the presentation Mr Major called for questions. After one enquiry about the impact on incomes of Labour's proposals, the prime minister looked around for further questions. He seemed surprised by the lack of interest. 'You are a very acquiescent lot this morning,' he commented.

As soon as Mr Major agreed to answer more general questions he was immediately challenged by Peter MacMahon, political editor of the *Sunday Mirror.* 'You said you had been jostled by a Labour mob in Bolton. Isn't that pathetic coming from someone who grew up on a soapbox? Aren't you running scared?' Mr Major denied complaining about being jostled. What concerned him was the sight of people making obscene gestures. He also rejected suggestions that his *Walden* interview had been brought forward, saying he had always intended it should be broadcast on the first Sunday of the campaign.

Each day the backdrop for the news conference was changed so as to illustrate the theme of the day. The main slogan was 'The Cost of Labour's Manifesto.' The capital 'L' was again a superimposed red L-plate, first featured on a poster unveiled at Torquay. Maurice Saatchi stood at the rear of the room surveying his agency's work.

Using the learner symbol to denigrate Labour proved controversial. Over 70% of learner drivers pass within a year and there were conflicting views over whether the poster was damaging to the Conservative campaign. Mr Saatchi said there was no evidence that people felt sympathy for learner drivers. 'We chose the learner symbol after the most comprehensive research ever undertaken for a political slogan. Our focus groups concluded that Labour were inexperienced, incompetent, unqualified and had never passed the test. Research by Harris showed that it was the most powerful political communication since the "Labour Isn't Working" poster.' Mr Saatchi said the L-plate symbol would be retained as a visual theme throughout the election.

Journalists leaving the news conference seemed confused about the story line. They felt Mr Lamont could just as easily have costed Labour's programme at £58 billion. One leading political editor described how Central Office were ringing political correspondents telling them the worst was over and that the prime minister was having a real impact on the campaign.

Mrs Thatcher was out on the hustings supporting her successor. Among the constituences she visited was the Conservative marginal of Dulwich where her vote was registered. She remained a doughty campaigner, refusing to get rattled when reporters told her that four of the five opinion polls for the Sunday newspapers put Labour ahead by up to five points. 'Can't you say something cheerful? If that is what the polls are saying, we will just have to get them right. It's early days yet.' Late that evening Central Office confirmed that Mrs Thatcher would join Mr Major the next day on the platform at the traditional candidates' meeting. There was no mention of this earlier when television and radio journalists were briefed about to-morrow's arrangements. We inevitably interpreted Mrs Thatcher's attendance as a last last minute move to toughen up the campaign.

SUNDAY 22 MARCH DAY 12

Thirteen years in government instilled a sense of supreme confidence in Conservative MPs and candidates. Some political correspondents felt this bordered on complacency. However, as a consequence, Tory gatherings were usually relatively relaxed affairs with no shortage of conspiratorial jokes. The tight regime exercised by Mr Kinnock, coupled with a deep desire for power, ensured far greater self discipline in the Labour and trade union movement. When on election parade, surrounded by potentially hostile journalists, Labour MPs were always careful never to crack jokes about Mr Kinnock, nor was there the merest hint of disloyalty to the leadership or to the party by the shadow cabinet.

Reporters milled around in the foyer of the Queen Elizabeth II conference centre as Tory representatives arrived for the candidates' meeting. The candidates' meeting is traditionally held by the Tories at the start of an election campaign, as a way of building up party morale. Philip Stephens, political editor of the *Financial Times*, who was wearing an open necked shirt, was teased by the Wolverhampton MP Nicholas Budgen: 'Are you trying to look like Val Doonican too?' Mr Stephens jovially reprimanded Mr Budgen: 'Now, now, no disloyalty to your leader.' There were already several Major jokes doing the rounds, including one circulated by a former Thatcher adviser to the effect that party officials were insisting Mr Major was tucked up in bed by 10.30 pm as otherwise they were not sure whether he would stay the course.

Tory press officers were decidedly unamused that morning, complaining that the Sunday newspapers were quite wrong to suggest that by bringing on Mrs Thatcher, the Conservatives were faltering and in a panic. 'Our friends on the Sundays have not been very helpful,' said Tim Collins, the party's press secretary. He would not expand on this cryptic remark. Mr Collins was a press officer for some months, transferring to the communications department from the employment secretary, Michael Howard's, office where he was a special adviser. He advanced rapidly, having started at Central Office in the research department. Colleagues regarded Mr Collins, who was in his late twenties, as something of a workaholic and there were a few envious mutterings when he was selected to be the press officer to accompany Mr Major during the campaign.

Thunderous applause greeted the prime minister and his predecessor as they walked together onto the platform. Chris Patten said that the organisers had made an exception at this candidates' meeting and asked a former prime minister to speak – something which did not usually happen – because Mrs Thatcher's achievements had to be safeguarded. I could not help thinking that Mrs Thatcher would hardly have allowed Ted Heath to speak at her candidates' meeting, or asked him to rally her troops for her.

Speaking off-the-cuff, without notes, Mrs Thatcher electrified her audience. She was applauded repeatedly, roundly rejecting the notion that the two parties were lookalikes. The essence of the socialist creed was to impose more government control over people's lives. 'That's why they love that socialist Delors' socialist charter. When will they learn? You cannot build Jerusalem in Brussels.' Reporters seemed as bowled over as the candidates, wallowing in the nostalgia of a vintage Thatcher performance. I thought: 'If only Major could make a speech like that.'

Mrs Thatcher's pledge to fight with 'her most earnest endeavour' to get Mr Major returned to Downing Street was delivered with conviction. There was talk in the campaign team that Mrs Thatcher might become a loose cannon and go off unexpectedly, upstaging her successor. But she didn't. Party managers were delighted with her speech and the reception it received, their only regret being that they were forced to wait 15 months for this high profile hand over.

Mr Major, emboldened by the harmony, and determined not to be outdone, put new strength into his delivery. He said their manifesto built on Margaret's legacy. 'Don't just defend our record. Go out there and proclaim our record and be proud of it. It's changed the face of Britain.' Reporters crowded round the candidates as the meeting concluded, attempting to get some first hand impressions of progress in the campaign. Some of those questioned thought it was a risky strategy putting Mrs Thatcher up against Mr Major. But there was general agreement that after the public reconciliation they had just witnessed, there was no way the news media could drive a wedge between Thatcher and Major.

Norman Tebbit had none of the doubts he expressed at the manifesto launch. He told me: 'They certainly put something in John's tea this morning. It was risky putting him on after Margaret, rather like being asked to perform an aria after Maria Callas. But he did a good job. He's got some new speech writers, some of the guys who used to write for Margaret.'

The high profile role given to Mrs Thatcher was exploited by Labour. They were hoping to find a way of reawakening the voters' anger over the poll tax. Eighty per cent of households had either just received their poll tax demand, or were expecting it within days. Labour's environment spokesman Bryan Gould took delight in welcoming the readiness of Mr Major to embrace 'Mrs Poll Tax.'

David Hill was convinced that the Thatcher endorsement would only remind electors that she was still the backseat driver. 'Obviously the 35% of voters who are committed Tories love her. But the other 65% are terrified. It would have been hard to think up a more badly timed reminder of the poll tax. Don't the Tories realise every move like this gets exaggerated because they are on the run?'

Labour definitely benefited from what was obviously a period of deep introspection for Conservative newspapers as they tried to work out an editorial line to express their divided loyalties between Thatcher and Major. Phil Woolas, whose job it was to come up with news stories and photo-opportunities to counter Tory publicity, was surprised by how little flak Labour were getting from the Tory tabloids. 'We are amazed how easy it has been. All the enquiries we are getting from Tory papers are pretty small beer so far. We thought they would try to ambush us all the time.'

There was also a high degree of satisfaction at the Liberal Democrats' headquarters. Olly Grender, the senior media officer, said there was no sign of Paddy Ashdown being squeezed. 'We haven't had to complain any more than we usually do. In fact we are very pleased with the amount of time we are getting on television and radio. According to our monitoring, the Liberal Democrats' share is very reasonable.'

As the day wore on there was a noticeable cooling in the afterglow created by the ecstatic reception for Mrs Thatcher. In an interview for *The World This Weekend* the former Tory communications director Brendan Bruce criticised Central Office's news management for having created an 'unfortunate perception' about Mrs Thatcher's intervention. Her speech had in fact been arranged well in advance, but by allowing the news media to imply it was a last minute invitation, Mr Bruce thought Central Office reinforced the impression that the Conservatives' campaign was not going well.

Chris Patten personally supervised the release of the news. He gave the information out in advance, exclusively, at an unattributable Friday lobby briefing at which access is restricted to political correspondents on Sunday newspapers. The Sunday lobby, as it is known, is used regularly by political leaders of all parties as a way of passing on news stories which they hope will be prominently displayed in the Sunday newspapers. In return for the journalists' implied promise of extensive coverage, politicians agree to the exclusion of reporters from news agencies, television and radio.

Because of Mr Patten's reliance on the Sunday lobby, television and radio journalists only found out about Mrs Thatcher's intended speech on Saturday evening, when they saw early editions of the Sunday newspapers. The headlines seemed capable of only one interpretation. 'Faltering Tories turn to Thatcher,' said *The Independent on Sunday*. *The Observer* had: 'Major plays the Thatcher card.'

By late Sunday evening Mr Patten looked as though he had been hit by a 'double whammy' himself. He felt he had been taken for a ride by the Sunday newspapers and then humiliated. 'Those headlines were just dishonest. I told the Sunday lobby that Margaret was on the agenda for weeks. They kept carrying on at us to keep it as a Sunday exclusive and then look what they do.' Mr Patten was in no mood to take any more and when I gently suggested that it was rather odd to give exclusives to the Sunday newspaper lobby when his party was fighting a television election, he simply closed his eyes.

DAY 13 MONDAY 23 MARCH

WEEK 3 – 17 DAYS TO GO

At the start of the campaign Chris Patten appeared to enjoy the task of chairing the Conservatives' news conferences. His daily jousts with political correspondents were conducted with scholarly aplomb. At the manifesto launch he gently chided one journalist for embarking on a lengthy supplementary, saying the briefing was a question and answer session not a Socratic dialogue. Another reporter, who had inquired whether the Tory campaign had started 'to falter,' was told he would probably get through his Thesaurus pretty quickly if he tried changing his verbs with every opinion poll.

By the start of the third week the bonhomie evaporated. The chairman had developed a Jekyll and Hyde personality. Gone were the droll comments of previous news conferences. Taking their place were snide observations. For some reason Mr Patten decided it was time to start baiting the journalists.

Labour's tax plans had been chosen by the Conservatives as the subject for their opening news conference of the third week. Another new poster was pasted on the wall, a reworking of an earlier advertisement attacking 'Labour's tax bombshell.' Among the journalists taking their seats was Anthony Bevins, political editor of *The Independent*. Mr Bevins has a long established reputation as a fearless questioner. He is well known at Westminster and most politicians are only too conscious of the danger of needlessly provoking him.

Mr Patten led Mr Major on to the platform and opened up the proceedings. On inviting questions Mr Patten looked at Mr Bevins: 'It's going to be your day in a moment Tony, provided you ask only one question.' This produced titters on the platform. Mr Major smiled. Mr Patten rubbed in the point: 'I will call Michael Brunson of ITN first and then Tony, for his one question.'

At the appropriate moment Mr Bevins asked the prime minister to give a pledge not to increase the tax burden in the next parliament. Mr Major said direct taxes had come down substantially in recent years and the country could be certain that the burden of taxation would rise under Labour. By now other journalists were ready for the chase, challenging Mr Major to explain why the tax burden had increased under 13 years of Conservative government. The prime minister walked straight into the trap: 'Well it isn't accurate. The tax burden is broadly flat...' At this point Mr Major was interrupted by shouts from the journalists: 'No, no that's not true.'

Mr Bevins was at the forefront of those protesting. Mr Major tried again: 'Tony is taking as his basis the level of tax in 1978–1979 against the borrowing requirement which was not met by taxation.' Mr Bevins suggested Mr Major should look at his own borrowing requirement because it was bigger than the Conservatives inherited from Labour. Mr Patten, sensing he had lost control of the news conference, tried to interrupt: 'I am sure that as a proportion...' The rest of the chairman's answer was drowned in further protests. Mr Bevins waved a treasury paper repeating his assertion that the Conservatives now had a larger borrowing requirement. Again Mr Patten tried unsuccessfully to restore order. The prime minister smiled wanly. He realised he was on his own: 'Yes, I have answered the question three times. The burden is broadly flat. The tax burden under Labour would rise dramatically.'

Most journalists looked on in disbelief during this exchange. The comparisons were obvious and immediate. In their day Mrs Thatcher and her press secretary Sir Bernard Ingham would have brooked no interruption. At the height of the Thatcher years they were a formidable duo. Sir Bernard knew just how to deflate an awkward questioner and Mrs Thatcher would move in instantly for the kill. They regularly made mincemeat of provocative political correspondents, but tended to avoid gratuitous insults unless they were needed. As Mr Major walked off the platform after the news conference he was pursued by Mr Bevins who was still brandishing his treasury paper, attempting to attract the prime minister's attention. The ferocity of the incident, and Mr Major's failure to deal with it effectively, stunned many of the party workers who were in the room. At a second press conference that afternoon some of the staff were still agitated. Political correspondents sensed that while the Tories were on the defensive it was a good moment for some probing questions.

Among those pressed for an explanation on the apparent disarray was Andrew Lansley, director of the Conservative research department. He insisted that the Conservatives' counter attack on Labour's tax plans was working, but said that from now on their campaign would be directed away from middle and upper income families, who were largely pro-Tory anyway, and would be retargeted at the skilled working class. 'Obviously we in the Tory party – here at Central Office – have been caught off guard by John Smith's shadow budget, just like everybody else, but not for long. It will explode in Labour's face. Our campaign will concentrate on the fact that tax, prices and mortgages would have to go up under Labour.'

Mr Lansley acknowledged that the party was facing presentational problems. 'What the prime minister didn't realise was how much of the campaign rests on him. Two-thirds of all the visual emphasis has to be contributed by Mr Major himself.' His observation underlined one of the greatest difficulties for the Conservatives. Because of security, very few details were given out in advance about where cabinet ministers would be campaigning. The lack of information led to complaints to the party's deputy head of media, Michael Gunton, who was responsible for briefing the regional press.

In an attempt to provide at least some guidance Mr Gunton arranged for copies of a daily campaign diary to be handed out at every news conference. However, this indicated only the name of a region to be toured by a cabinet minister and instead of providing an established regional breakdown, the list gave area names used by Conservative and Unionist Associations.

Journalists were left to decipher the cryptic clues on the list. For example, according to Central Office, the area designated only as 'Wessex' meant Buckinghamshire and Oxfordshire as well as Hampshire, Dorset and Wiltshire. Newsroom staff, trying to plan future coverage, found the lists were virtually useless. Their only solution was to ring the area offices themselves. Far more extensive lists, complete with precise times and locations, were issued by both Labour and the Liberal Democrats.

Later, after his bruising encounter at the morning news conference, the prime minister faced further tough questioning over the trade figures which showed a current account deficit in February of £750 million compared with city expectations of £450 million. Mr Major insisted that exports were up. He was also reminded on *The World At One* that no prime minister for 30 years had come from behind in the opinion polls and won an election. Mr Major was rattled, refusing, as he put it, to waste his time talking about opinion polls. Journalists accompanying Mr Major had a frustrating day, unable to get sight of him for over six hours. For much of the afternoon Mr Major remained closeted in a private house, preparing his speech for a rally that evening.

The day's most memorable event involved Mrs Thatcher. On a walk-about near Stockport she was attacked with a bunch of daffodils. A woman approached her apparently offering the flowers. As Mrs Thatcher went to accept the flowers, the woman began flailing them at the ex-prime minister's head. Mrs Thatcher appeared unruffled, delivering the best one-liner of the day: 'It was so hard on the daffodils.'

Labour party strategists were beginning to think they were heading inexorably for victory on polling day, and the opinion polls supported their optimism. There certainly was every indication that although Labour might not actually be winning the election, the Conservatives were in the process of losing it. Labour was not making the mistakes or blunders predicted, nor were any gaffes being made by Neil Kinnock, the principal target of the Tory tabloids. Nevertheless there was no sign of the press pack giving up the hunt. Reporters from the popular papers remained confident that the latter stages of the campaign were much more likely to be dominated by personalities than policies.

By week three an invitation to attend the preview of yet another election broadcast hardly seemed a promising assignment. The latest party political was designed to launch a new Labour offensive attacking the government's record on the national health service. There was speculation for some days about the timing of a switch to health, which the opinion polls indicated was Labour's strongest issue. Labour kept the government on the defensive over the recession but eventually decided to change tack and the plan was to use the third week of the campaign to promote their plans for increased spending on health and education.

Health was bound to be a flashpoint between Labour and the Conservatives. John Major gave repeated assurances that the service would not be privatised, but Labour were relentless in exploiting public uncertainty. While the government continued to give approval for hospitals to opt out of the NHS management structure and acquire trust status, Labour could go on claiming that this amounted to privatisation.

Labour's health spokesman, Robin Cook, has a formidable record for harrying the government and he is an astute manipulator of the news media, having carefully timed the release of a succession of leaked NHS documents to create maximum impact. On the day the election was called Labour backed Mr Cook's forceful campaigning with newspaper advertisements telling the dramatic story of the death of a child aged 18 months.

Below a snapshot of a smiling baby girl were two large headlines: 'Georgina Norris died because the NHS is short of money. Meanwhile, the Tories are cutting taxes to keep their election hopes alive.' The advertisement alleged that two operations for Georgina, who had had a serious heart condition, were cancelled, and when she was finally treated, as an emergency, it was too late. Great Ormond Street Hospital challenged Labour's account of her death. Her operation was delayed due to an unusual number of emergencies and not because of a lack of funds. The health secretary William Waldegrave accused Labour of sinking to new depths. A front page headline in the *Daily Mail* described it as 'Labour's First Dirty Trick.'

William Waldegrave said, when discussing the prospect of a new health offensive with Chris Pattern, that he was waiting for Labour to start 'parading dead children again.' On display, as a backdrop at Labour's health briefing, was a blow up of their latest campaign advertisement. Beneath a picture of a plastic credit card were the words: 'Tory Health Policy. More Plastic Surgeons.' Labour handed out copies of letters from patients who described how they were forced into paying for private treatment because NHS waiting lists were so long. This was the message Labour intended to underline.

Set to B B King's soulful blues number *Someone Really Loves You*, the broadcast opened with the words: 'The story of two girls with the same problem ... one can afford private treatment, the other can't.' Both had excruciating earache and needed surgery. One mother was told her daughter would have to wait nine months for an operation. The second girl, from a wealthier family, would have her treatment quickly because her mother was able to pay. The broadcast intercut between the experiences of the two girls. There were harrowing scenes showing the discomfort of the girl who had to wait, while the second mother was shown writing a cheque for £200.

Mike Newell, who made the film *Dance With a Stranger*, about the life of Ruth Ellis, the last woman to be hanged in the UK, directed the broadcast. Actresses were used throughout, but Labour insisted it was consistent with an actual case.

After the briefing Mr Cook said the story line was prompted by a letter from the father of a girl who had waited 11 months for treatment for an ear infection. 'We are not releasing the name of the girl or her parents, but I can assure you that the case was based on the letter received from the father.' When pressed to give further details Mr Cook refused, but he insisted there was not a single case which he had publicised where he had been proved wrong in any substantial fact.

Once the briefing finished there was an immediate buzz of excitement. The broadcast was extremely distressing. It was uncomfortable watching a young girl in such pain. Her tears and runny nose left me feeling that surgeons doing private treatment were villains. I could not remember when I had last seen such an emotive appeal from the Labour party. It verged on class war propaganda: the contrast between health care for rich and poor children was gigantic. I could tell it had the same effect on some of the other journalists. 'If this story doesn't stand up, Labour are for it,' said one reporter. I joined in the attempts to cross question Labour press officers about the identity of the girl, but we got nowhere.

Labour's campaign director, Jack Cunningham, was equally resolute: he refused to give more details. He made no apology for using a sick child to make a political point. 'Labour isn't looking for these stories. They're being brought to us because of people's everyday experiences.'

Although Mr Cook and Dr Cunningham held the line in London, at a second briefing in Manchester for those journalists who were accompanying Mr Kinnock, his press officer, Julie Hall, revealed that the girl's name was Jennifer. Miss Hall had with her letters from the father and the hospital consultant from which she read extracts. However, she did not reveal the family's surname, the identity of the consultant, or give any clue as to where Jennifer lived.

After the first transmission of the broadcast at 6.55 pm on ITV, William Waldegrave accused Labour of scraping the barrel by implying that no child had ever gone without hospital care while Labour were in power. 'I think the broadcast is ruthless. I think it's wicked. There is so much the British people will put up with, and then they will say "no more." I think Labour have gone too far.'

At the start of the campaign Mr Waldegrave wrote to national newspaper editors telling them to beware of dubious case histories paraded by Labour. He impressed on me the need for the action he took. 'I told the editors to watch it. Every newspaper does its own investigations and sometimes they are not right. I reminded them not to take as fact Labour case histories publicised in the *Daily Mirror* because they often turn out to be wrong.'

Labour's attempt to open up a new offensive on health produced a lively exchange between Jeremy Paxman and Mr Major on *Newsnight*. The prime minister assured Mr Paxman that the NHS would remain free at the point of delivery and that no further charges would be introduced. Mr Major had seen the NHS at close quarters throughout his life. 'I saw it treat my parents through years of illness, I've seen my children born on the NHS, I've been treated myself on the NHS, I am committed to the NHS and I am going to build up the NHS in the way we have built it up in the past.'

Because Mr Major was visiting Scotland the interview had to be pre-recorded in Edinburgh three hours before transmission. In the hope of securing publicity for the programme, reporters were invited to watch the discussion as it came down the line and was fed into the BBC television centre in London. *Newsnight's* transmission time of 10.30 pm is too late for many newspaper editions and a dozen journalists had taken up the offer to watch the interview so that they could file early copy on Mr Major's remarks. To begin with they could only see Mr Paxman sitting in a room in the Caledonian Hotel.

When Mr Major arrived there were the usual opening pleasant-ries. Mr Paxman checked voice levels by enquiring if Mr Major ever had time for food. After saying he was managing to eat 'from time to time, but not a lot' Mr Major asked if he could be given something to strengthen his cushion. He was sitting in a comfortable looking upright armchair. Mr Major said that a book would do. Mr Paxman seemed slightly thrown by this: 'A book? Won't that be uncomfort-able?' Mr Major insisted a book would suffice. 'I have a bad back. If I sink into the chair it makes it uncomfortable.'

Journalists in London, already transfixed by the conversation, watched with fascination as Mr Major joined in efforts to bolster the cushion. At one point the prime minister could be seen fumbling with it saying: 'That's no good.' Then a second cushion was produced. After a further short delay the interview started. Because of a leg injury and back trouble Mr Major had asked before to sit on firm chairs, especially during lengthy questioning by reporters on tiring foreign trips.

The arrangement for Mr Paxman's interview to be conducted in a hotel room was made by the Conservative party. Sue Robertson, *Newsnight's* political producer, who regularly sets up interviews with politicians, told me she was surprised that Mr Major's cam-paign staff had apparently not taken the precaution of checking his chair before the interview started. She knew from bitter experience that chairs could be the bane of a producer's life.

Before joining the BBC Miss Robertson was secretary to the parliamentary committee of the Social Democratic party and press officer to its former leader Dr David Owen. 'Whenever I arranged a television interview for Dr Owen, I always had to make sure he had a chair with arms. Without them he felt uncomfortable and didn't know where to put his arms and hands. When Roy Jenkins spoke in public he liked to rest his notes on a lectern and that had to be carted round the country. This might make political leaders sound insecure, but as they are under such pressure and because presentation is so important, I considered it an integral part of a press officer's job to make sure they had what they needed.'

While Mr Paxman was conducting his interview in Edinburgh, Labour's press office in London was becoming increasingly alarmed at the scale of the reaction to the election broadcast on what had by now been dubbed 'the saga of Jennifer's ear.' David Hill, the director of communications, was determined to remain calm when I spoke to him on the telephone. 'We knew our broadcast would create a certain degree of journalistic activity. But we stand by our message. The case we depicted is representative of what is happening in the health service.' Labour assumed that the response to the broadcast was simply another indication that the party's campaign was continuing to break new ground.

Among those advising on Labour's campaign and communications strategies was Patricia Hewitt, Mr Kinnock's press secretary until her appointment as deputy director of the Institute for Public Policy Research. After three years' work as a think-tank of the left, the Institute gained a place at the forefront of future Labour thinking.

Miss Hewitt told me she thought the Conservatives' election tactics were looking more and more like a carbon copy of Labour's 1987 campaign on which she had worked with Mr Kinnock. 'We used question and answer sessions with Neil in 1987 but we didn't do anything as silly as put him on a bar stool, and he did face real questions. Major has now repeated Neil's famous 'I warn you . . .' speech from the 1987 election campaign, and they've even done a movie, stealing, as we did, from the classics. Even though we lost in 1987, we had all the good campaign ideas and now the Conservatives are pinching them, but I don't think they are reproducing them very well.' Her satisfaction summed up the cautious, but nevertheless confident, mood I detected among other members of Labour's campaign team.

DAY 15 WEDNESDAY 25 MARCH

Labour's 'Jennifer's ear' broadcast was front page news in some of the national newspapers. *Today* reproduced stills of the girl's agonised face and her distraught mother with the headline: 'Pain, Tears, Politics.' A report in *The Independent* named the girl as Jennifer Bennett and quoted Alan Ardouin, a consultant at the Kent and Canterbury Hospital, saying that surgery was delayed by an administrative error. The *Daily Express* carried the banner headline: 'Exposed: Labour's Sick NHS Stunts.' On BBC's *Breakfast News* William Waldegrave claimed that the techniques Labour had used 'wouldn't have been out of place in pre-war Germany.'

Robin Cook was hoping the broadcast would act as a curtain raiser for the publication of Labour's health budget. One of the spending plans revealed the previous week was an extra £1 billion for the NHS. Although the presentation was impressive, with Mr Cook announcing additional money to purchase new ambulances and boost the employment of nurses and junior doctors, the news conference lacked the authority of John Smith's budget launch. No longer did Labour seem to convey the certainty of becoming the next government which had struck me so forcefully the previous week. Overshadowing the proceedings was the saga of Jennifer's ear.

Journalists enquired whether young girls were forced to seek private treatment under the last Labour government. Mr Cook parried the questions. He could not give a guarantee that from 10 April no one would have to wait for an operation. As Neil Kinnock left the platform he was followed by reporters demanding to know whether the broadcast amounted to 'the big lie.' The Labour leader retorted: 'We are telling the big truth.'

Among those pursuing Mr Kinnock was Peter Hitchens of the *Daily Express*. His report claiming Labour's broadcast was a 'fraud' was given the tag 'exclusive.' I first knew Mr Hitchens during the 1980s when he was well known on the industrial beat for his persistence in questioning trade union leaders. He was in Moscow during the Soviet coup. Colleagues suggested mischieviously that the real reason Gorbachov finally stepped down was to escape Mr Hitchens's persistent questioning.

Political correspondents, who were being accommodated during the week at the Royal Horseguards Hotel, were surprised that morning to see Mr Hitchens in the lift. They enquired why he had come back from Moscow. He gave a one word answer: 'Kinnock.' Later, in a statement, Labour accused Mr Hitchens of playing the angry reporter. 'He crashed through a crowd and put a tape recorder in front of Mr Kinnock. Neil put his arm round Mr Hitchens's shoulder and said: "Let's talk about it." Neil was perfectly calm. It was an exercise in trying to create an incident.'

As the press pack left for the Conservatives' news conference, we were divided about the effectiveness of Labour's broadcast. However, Alastair Campbell, political editor of the *Daily Mirror*, told me he was in no doubt it had scored a bull's eye. 'Labour are just loving all the attention. It keeps health right at the top of the agenda.'

At Central Office there was a somewhat subdued response to begin with. Mr Patten was decidedly restrained. He considered the broadcast revealed more about Labour's ethics than the dedication of NHS workers. Party strategists were clearly in a dilemma. Opinion poll research suggested the Conservatives suffered whenever health was pushed up the news agenda because voters had greater trust in Labour on health. Bob Worcester, chairman of MORI, had queried Conservative tactics on previous occasions, wondering how many times the Tories would go on banging their heads against the wall of the NHS before realising 'they couldn't knock it over.'

I sensed that the communications team was anxious for the Conservative news conference to finish. We were encouraged to assemble outside as quickly as possible for a 'strong visual message.' Maurice Saatchi told television crews there would soon be some good pictures. Laid out on the pavement was a large wooden model of a factory. Written on the chimneys were the words 'investment', 'jobs' and 'recovery.' No sooner were the television cameras in place than a steamroller trundled into Smith Square. Its livery was funereal, painted black. The only splash of colour was a red L-plate of the kind featured in the Saatchi and Saatchi posters. The steamroller proceeded to smash the wooden model to smithereens, stopping only a few feet short of the front door of Central Office. Tory press and broadcasting officers thought the stunt hilarious. My immediate thought was that Shaun Woodward's experience must have been invaluable: it was just the kind of jape *That's Life* would have been proud of.

Sean Holden, the Conservatives' head of broadcasting, told me that the visual and audio impact would be great on television and radio. 'We are trying to talk to the C2s and this will get the message across to them that their jobs are at risk if Labour get elected.' Mr Holden used to be a political reporter with TV-am. As he was speaking a large shroud was being thrown hurriedly over what remained of the factory. I could see that his colleagues had become concerned because photographers were trying to line up shots of the smashed words 'investment,' 'jobs' and 'recovery.' The press officers lacked Mr Holden's conviction. They feared newspaper pictures of a shattered factory might give the wrong impression.

Meanwhile in Smith Square a second drama was unfolding. I walked over to join Anthony Bevins, political editor of *The Independent*, who was inquiring about the political affiliation of the steamroller's driver. The man looked embarrassed. He looked down at us and said: 'I am just doing my job. Now mind your feet.' After the steamroller backed out into Smith Square we noticed Saatchi's red L-plate fixed to the front. When we asked if the driver had passed his test he had clearly had enough and ran off round the corner. A police constable nearby told me he was not interested in an unattended steamroller nor in the fact that it had no number plate. 'We have to make allowances for all sorts of things in elections.'

Mr Patten missed the fun, preferring to stay inside Central Office. A BBC television crew was waiting to film his departure for Bath where he was due to spend the afternoon campaigning.

Mr Patten's driver emerged with the chairman's bag, but was suddenly recalled. Another episode was about to unfold in the saga of Jennifer's ear, upstaging the steamroller and its carefully contrived photo-opportunity. Within minutes the BBC crew was invited inside to film an interview with Mr Patten who read from a statement issued by Jennifer Bennett's grandfather, Peter Lee-Roberts, a former Conservative mayor. He accused Labour of telling lies and said the doctors were marvellous. Once the hospital realised his granddaughter was a priority she had the operation within weeks.

Mr Patten claimed the grandfather's account proved Labour's broadcast was the 'very worst imaginable example of political sleaze.' Now he had a way to pin responsibility onto Mr Kinnock because at the end of the 'Jennifer's ear' broadcast the Labour leader indicated that he wanted every child to have the best in health care and not to be dependent upon the amount their parents could pay. Jennifer's grandfather's statement confirmed the Conservatives' stand that the NHS *was* working and that money was not the issue.

Mr Kinnock was asked to apologise for his remarks. By now the Tory chairman was in full flood. BBC political news organiser Joy Johnson noticed that rather than keeping his eye on the interviewer, Mr Patten was looking directly into the camera, making a direct appeal to the viewers. He said Mr Kinnock's failure to check the facts made him unfit to be prime minister. 'If, in order to grub for office, you don't give a hang for the truth, then I think you disqualify yourself from the trust and respect which those who try for the highest office in the country should seek to earn.'

Afterwards Mr Patten's press officer Angie Bray confirmed that the chairman had cancelled his constituency visit. There was too much happening in London. Miss Bray shared Mr Patten's anger.

She was press officer when the Conservatives lost the Monmouth by election the previous May. The defeat was blamed on the 'big lie' spread by Labour that a local hospital was about to be privatised. I knew how much this irked her. 'At last Labour have been caught out,' she said.

News bulletins were reporting signs of conflict inside the Bennett family. Jennifer's father, John Bennett, who wrote to Mr Cook and described himself as a floating voter, was pleased that Labour's broadcast had put the spotlight on hospital waiting lists. But Margaret Bennett, Jennifer's mother, who was a Conservative and had written about Jennifer's case to the local Tory MP, said her daughter's experience was quite different from that portrayed on television. 'I would never have given permission for the Labour party to use my child as a political football.'

Shaun Woodward believed that the disrepancies which were emerging from Labour's 'Jennifer's ear' broadcast were so serious that they had given the Conservatives the breakthrough they were looking for. His optimism was shared by Richard Ryder, the government's chief whip, who stopped to speak for a few moments as he rushed into Central Office. 'This is a terrible day for Labour. This could be the turning point in the election.' Mr Patten, by remaining in London, was able to take the chair at a second news conference. He renewed his charge that Mr Kinnock was so desperate to hold office, he would say anything to get into Downing Street.

Mr Patten's criticisms provoked more riveting exchanges with journalists. It seemed to me that the chairman had just been waiting to get his own back after Monday's confrontation on Labour's tax plans. When Anthony Bevins suggested that if all politicians were hanged for the truth there would not be many serious office holders left, Mr Patten told him to listen to the facts. On running through a list of Conservative achievements on health, Mr Patten noticed Mr Bevins was not writing anything in his notebook. 'So fascinating are these facts, Tony, I see you don't even bother to take them down. I hope they will be reported in your great and independent organ.'

Previous entreaties to journalists to avoid a Socratic dialogue were thrown asunder when Michael White, political editor of *The Guardian*, incurred the chairman's wrath for accusing the Conservatives of being just as guilty as Labour of shroud waving. Mr Patten replied: 'No, no. In the winter of discontent we could have produced one cancer patient after another who was suffering from the activities of left wing public service unions: we didn't do that.'

White: 'I have a distinct recollection that you did.'

Patten: 'You try to find a broadcast. You won't find one. You won't find an example of us fabricating the facts like Labour.'

White: 'You benefit from the Tory tabloids who do it for you.'

Patten: 'I wouldn't be so sanctimonious about that if I were you. Even the broadsheets are not perfect.'

White: 'We are not. We are grubbing for circulation and you are grubbing for votes.'

Patten: 'Not grubbing for votes.'

White: 'I have sat here in this room and heard some whoppers.'

Patten: 'And I have had some whoppers put to me.'

Mr Patten seemed oblivious to the television cameras recording this unexpected altercation. He agreed at the conclusion of questions that his spat with Mr White made him appear more passionate than usual. He promised his 'normal, calm mood' would return. However, I could not help thinking that Mr Patten had again undermined his role as chairman of the news conferences. His great strength on such occasions was his ability to engage in pleasant and witty dialogue. The importance of this to John Major and his colleagues is that it helps defuse tension and, more importantly, gives the minister concerned a few vital seconds to think up a neat answer.

Immediately the Conservatives' news conference finished journalists hurried to a briefing by Jack Cunningham. Labour handed out copies of a letter from Alan Ardouin, Jennifer's consultant at the Kent and Canterbury Hospital. In the letter Mr Ardouin told the girl's father that the delay in her operation was due to an unacceptable increase in the hospital's waiting list caused by 'insufficient funding.' Dr Cunningham said Labour's broadcast had been completely exonerated by Mr Ardouin's explanation. 'This exposes the hypocrisy of Patten and Waldegrave. Their attempts to turn this into a personal attack on Neil Kinnock are contemptible. They want to challenge the integrity and honesty of Labour in a desperate attempt to deflect attention from long waiting lists.'

However, Labour had clearly been wrongfooted and taken by surprise. It was clear to me there had been no prior assessment about what to do if the broadcast did backfire. Either the party should have shredded all reference to the name Jennifer the moment the broadcast was commissioned and said it was fictional but representative, or they should have been prepared to issue the correspondence immediately when challenged. By leaving it 24 hours before releasing Mr Ardouin's letter, Labour compounded the confusion.

David Hill was dismayed that the focus of attention was the Bennett family itself rather than hospital waiting lists. I could sense his disappointment that Labour's health budget had failed to gain the prominence which he'd intended. 'Obviously it has been a confusing day. But the Bennett story has produced a flood of similar examples. We now have details of more than 200 cases where patients have had to wait a considerable time.'

What struck me afterwards was that Mr Hill had no idea what might happen next in the convoluted story about Labour's 'Jennifer's ear' broadcast. I shared his feeling that the story still had plenty of mileage but, like him, I did not know what to expect next.

DAY 16 THURSDAY 26 MARCH

Inevitably there would be a day when all the careful stage management by the campaign managers would disintegrate, leaving the spin doctors floundering for explanations. (The mission of these doctors is to put their party's interpretation – or spin – onto a particular story: to try to manipulate journalists). The tangled tale of Jennifer's ear had all the ingredients: a family apparently at war with itself, yet prepared for that conflict to be aired in the news media. And, running parallel with the Bennetts' trauma was a fascinating story of political intrigue. The election campaign was about to turn into a whodunnit, as Labour and the Conservatives blamed each other for leaking the name, Jennifer Bennett.

Neil Kinnock was the first to be interrogated. At a news conference in Nottingham he tried to clear Labour of any involvement: 'I condemn without reservation whoever gave this little girl's name to the newspapers.' But Mr Kinnock was challenged by a reporter from *The Sun* who said that on Tuesday afternoon, at an off-the-record briefing, his press secretary, Julie Hall, had disclosed the name Jennifer. Mr Kinnock was greeted by a chorus of 'No, no, no' from journalists when he insisted that this contradicted his information.

When Mr Kinnock repeated his condemnation, Roy Hattersley interrupted the proceedings to say that Miss Hall intended making a personal statement. She was clearly angry and upset. After a somewhat confusing account of her earlier briefing she immediately confronted the assembled journalists: 'If you are saying from the briefing on Tuesday that you were able to reveal the identity of the child and the family, it is you who have done that. The adult who did that should come up and admit it now.'

Miss Hall said her belief in the health service was the reason she was hoping to work for a Labour government. Her voice almost breaking, she recounted how as a student her father had paid for her to have private treatment for an eye complaint. 'My father could pay. He had the choice. Unfortunately, there are people out there in the country who can't.' She repeated her appeal for an explanation as to how the one word Jennifer could have been responsible for the story in the *Daily Express*. Significantly at this stage, Miss Hall didn't refer to the fact that the surname Bennett also appeared in *The Independent* that morning.

As Miss Hall walked away from the platform, a *Sunday Express* reporter, Bruce Anderson, appeared to be attracting her attention. Mr Kinnock saw this and called out: 'Julie, don't give that man the benefit of any form of conversation. He is simply not big enough.'

Tory newspapers were provided with the kind of spectacle they could previously only have dreamed about. There could hardly have been a moment when a political leader was upstaged so comprehensively by a press officer. Nor could I recall an occasion when the sight of Mr Kinnock losing his cool had been immortalised so clearly on television.

Miss Hall certainly threw caution to the wind as she stepped forward to make her statement. So great was her emotion in the heat of the moment that she seemed oblivious to the impact she was having on Mr Kinnock. Her decision to leave ITN and become his press officer was a matter of great personal pride for the Labour leader. I had heard frequent accounts from within the party that Mr Kinnock was pleased to introduce Miss Hall as an example of the good that could come out of the unprincipled world of journalism.

Few contemporary politicians have had to endure anything like the sustained savaging inflicted on Mr Kinnock in his eight-and-a-half years as leader of the opposition. He developed an unparalleled degree of resilience to the smears and ridicule to which he was subjected in the right wing press. But I feel that political correspondents paid a heavy price for the activities of the 'Get-Kinnock Tendency.' Access to Mr Kinnock has become so carefully controlled that in the run up to the election he rarely indulged in the informal question and answer sessions which journalists so appreciate. From the start of the campaign there were complaints by some reporters that Mr Kinnock was being over protected. His advisers believed they had no alternative but to limit the occasions when he came into direct personal contact with newspaper journalists.

Miss Hall's emotional statement had a spectacular impact on the journalists who witnessed it. Few could recall a moment when newshounds were so angry with each other; when dog would so savagely eat dog. The minute the news conference concluded the fearless *Daily Express* reporter, Peter Hitchens, found himself surrounded by reporters demanding to know how he had discovered the surname Bennett.

The interrogation was led by the *Daily Mirror's* political correspondent David Bradshaw. Mr Hitchens maintained that his leak was secondhand and that 'the source of the information came from within the Labour party campaign.' Refusing to go any further he rounded on Mr Bradshaw for having bawled and barked so ferociously that it looked as if someone had 'accidentally plugged him into national grid.' Within a short space of time every political correspondent in the country had joined the hue and cry. However, foregoing the usual newspaper rivalry, Sir Nicholas Lloyd, editor of the *Daily Express*, suggested that *The Independent* had in fact been first with the name, having obtained it from Labour. Although agreeing that they were first, *The Independent* said the information came from their own journalistic sources.

While the national newspapers were preoccupied in claim and counter claim, regional and local political correspondents were discovering that Labour's media planners were compounding their previous presentational errors over the Bennett case. Earlier that morning Labour issued the names and telephone numbers of nine patients whose operations had been postponed due to long hospital waiting lists. Several were offered private treatment because of the delays. Journalists were invited to contact the patients and publicise their cases. When the details were checked by local reporters discrepancies began to emerge. One of the patients claimed she had never sought publicity.

Labour's whole approach towards the publication of individual case histories was becoming decidedly cavalier. At one stage in the preparation of the 'Jennifer's ear' broadcast there was a possibility that it might have included a sound track recorded by Jennifer's father. Yet, as events were proving, the Bennett family was not in total agreement about the wisdom of publicising Jennifer's case.

Party workers had selected the names of the nine patients from the 200 cases which had emerged after the broadcast. But the only check was to ring back the people concerned. At no stage had they been visited to see if their stories were correct. Nor did the party know whether the patients or their families would be able to withstand the pressures which can result from exposure in the news media. The weakness of Labour's position became very apparent when Dr Cunningham and Mr Cook called journalists to an afternoon news conference. Their intention was to try to turn the debate back to Labour's plans for increased health spending, but regional reporters insisted on clarification about the position of the nine patients. Dr Cunningham looked rattled. He had obviously not expected Labour's list of patients awaiting NHS treatment to backfire in this way.

Mr Cook was also the target of pointed questions. He tried some diversionary tactics. The night before, at a rally in Wolverhampton, he revealed that, like Chris Patten, he had a predilection for goading reporters: he had interrupted his speech to enquire whether he was speaking too fast for Jon Craig, a political correspondent with the *Daily Express*, who was one of the reporters in the audience. On seeing that Mr Craig was also at this news conference, Mr Cook reminded him that the *Daily Express* had yet to report how Labour would devote an extra £1 billion to the health service. But point scoring got nowhere. Labour were on the defensive.

Politicians who instantly accused the news media of inaccuracy and a failure to check facts, were now beginning to look just as guilty. I thought it was about time Labour were exposed: they were publicising personal case histories for political gain but neglecting to check their facts. Their protestations about journalistic misconduct in the Bennett case were starting to look hypocritical. Under persistent questioning Dr Cunningham admitted that Labour had now apologised to one of the nine patients whose name was released that morning.

Labour's discomfort was about to be repeated at Central Office. I joined a crush of reporters eager to discover whether the Conservatives had played a role in leaking Jennifer's name. Lined up for a pre-arranged news conference was a group of medical professionals brought to London to give support to the government's health service reforms. Consultants, anaesthetists and general practitioners were sitting in serried ranks along one side of the room. As the health secretary William Waldegrave started to list the government's achievements, his parliamentary secretary Stephen Dorrell stepped forward to pull down posters revealing the revelant statistics. A hospital doctor and two surgeons gave their reasons for supporting hospital trusts. They claimed the new management system was more sensitive to patient needs. But the journalists were impatient. There was an immediate flurry of questions. Were the Conservatives the source of the leak?

Mr Waldegrave did not parry the questions as I expected he would, instead he stopped us all dead in our tracks: Jennifer's consultant Alan Ardouin had telephoned Tory party headquarters shortly before the broadcast, expressing concern over what Labour intended to say. 'We advised the consultant that if he wanted to pursue this matter, a good thing to do would be to contact a newspaper that might be interested. Nothing wrong with that at all.'

Mr Waldegrave's confirmation that the Conservatives had not only been in discussion with the consultant but had also told him to contact a newspaper, clearly had enormous implications. John Major and Chris Patten made no mention of the Conservatives' prior knowledge in their denunciations of Neil Kinnock over his unfitness to be prime minister. I saw that the possible consequences of this admission were beginning to assume devastating proportions. Reporters clamoured for more details. Had there been a cover up? Mr Waldegrave looked flustered. He seemed taken aback by the impact of his own revelation. He kept repeating that at no point had the Conservatives known the girl's name nor had they leaked it. His answers failed to satisfy the journalists.

As the questions continued unabated Mr Waldegrave appeared to be on the point of losing control of the news conference. I glanced across at the rows of consultants and doctors. They were watching in amazement. They had clearly never expected to see a health secretary flounder so badly. Mr Waldegrave had put himself in an impossible position: he was trying to control an unruly briefing while at the same time think on his feet and avoid any further political embarrassment.

Virginia Bottomley, the health minister, intervened to support Mr Waldegrave's assertion that hundreds of doctors and patients were ringing Conservative headquarters expressing their support. 'Our switchboard is jammed with calls. We are getting hundreds of calls. But we don't reveal the identity of patients.' Her final words were lost amid jeers from some reporters. As the questioning became even rowdier Mr Waldegrave rapidly closed the news conference, rushing off the platform with Mrs Bottomley.

There was pandemonium as journalists rushed forward, insisting that party officials should answer their questions. I was with a group which had Sean Holden, the Conservatives' head of broadcasting, pinned against a Tory poster. We asked whether he could comment on reports that Jennifer's grandfather, the former Conservative mayor of Faversham, had also alerted Central Office by faxing them advance information about the broadcast. Mr Holden, ashen faced, denied having seen a fax. He managed to break free and rejoin Shaun Woodward who was trying to fend off questions in the main reception area. It was a seething scrum of reporters and television crews.

Mr Woodward began to explain that the consultant had tele-phoned Central Office at 6 pm to warn that Labour were planning a sensational broadcast. A junior press officer had taken the call. As Mr Woodward was speaking he realised he was being filmed from above by one of the television crews which had managed, obviously without permission, to get some way up the main staircase. Mr Woodward protested, telling the crew to come down, insisting that the briefing was off-the-record and not to be filmed.

I could not help thinking that *That's Life* would have jumped at off-the-wall footage of this calibre. Here was the Conservatives' director of communications playing a star role in a graphic sequence of shots. As he reeled under the pressure of the questioning, Mr Woodward must have twigged that he was in danger of repeating the upstaging of Mr Kinnock by his press secretary. Obviously fearing that television pictures of his own briefing might appear in news bulletins, back to back with Julie Hall, he hurried upstairs, out of sight of the cameras. With the departure of Mr Woodward and the rest of the communications team, we all paused for a moment wondering who to question next. In another corner, battling to escape was Patrick Rock, special adviser to Mr Patten. I could hear him shouting: 'We didn't give out the name. Ask the editor of *The Independent.'*

When Mr Rock succeeded in beating a hasty retreat, we caught sight of the ex-health minister Sir Barney Hayhoe. He was standing beside the lifts talking to Robin Oakley, political editor of *The Times* and its columnist Peter Riddell. On discovering that he had become the centre of attraction Sir Barney fulminated at the eavesdroppers, including myself, saying he was engaged in a private lobby briefing.

Despite the bedlam, one of the general practitioners stood his ground in the reception area, mesmerised by the maelstrom unfolding around him. As the commotion finally subsided, and the television crews packed up their equipment, he muttered something about having paid £120 to hire a locum so that he could attend the briefing and support Mr Waldegrave. Although angry at not being called to speak, it was not clear whether the doctor thought the afternoon's entertainment had been worth his locum's fee.

As the last of the reporters departed I saw Sam Anderson, the press office news messenger, looking relieved. He gave me a knowing smile. As a party employee he must have been privy to some pretty unusual goings on inside Central Office. The political correspondents certainly could not remember a Conservative news conference ending so acrimoniously. Two hours later newsrooms were faxed a statement confirming that Conservative Central Office had contacted the *Daily Express* after the consultant's telephone call at 6.15 pm the previous Tuesday. Mr Ardouin said he had been approached at 4 pm by *The Independent* who already knew Jennifer's name. He was concerned that Labour's broadcast might contain a serious distortion of the facts.

However, Central Office was not aware of the girl's name until the Wednesday morning when it was revealed in *The Independent* and then in the *Daily Express*. A fax from Jennifer's grandfather was received at party headquarters but it had not contained her name.

After all the excitement, this detailed confirmation seemed something of an anti-climax. Labour tried unsuccessfully to turn the heat on Mr Waldegrave, calling on him to resign. Mr Cook claimed the health secretary's position was untenable because he had incited professional misconduct by advising a hospital consultant to breach patient confidentiality and talk to the *Daily Express*. One question which remained unanswered was how *The Independent* obtained Jennifer's name but the editor, Andreas Whittam-Smith, insisted 'categorically' that it did not come from a political source. Finally the trail had gone cold.

DAY 17 FRIDAY 27 MARCH

After the tumultuous events of the previous two days, there were inevitably some loose ends in the Bennett affair which journalists thought worth pursuing. For once though, Labour and the Conservatives seemed to be in agreement, signalling a readiness to draw a line under what for both parties had been a damaging encounter. However, Neil Kinnock and John Major could not escape entirely from further questioning because their own conduct was under scrutiny. As his parting shot, Mr Kinnock declared that the integrity of the Tory party was 'nil' because of their complicity with the *Daily*

Express. When challenged again over the role of his press secretary, Mr Kinnock agreed that she was holding letters about Jennifer when first questioned by reporters. But he doubted whether a journalist could have sneaked a look over her shoulder because she was aware of 'one or two prying eyes' and took precautions to ensure no one was standing behind her.

If Mr Kinnock's assumption was correct, Miss Hall's naivety beggared belief. As I would readily attest myself, reporters learn how to read upside down. We have got into the habit in such situations, when approached by officials carrying documents, of quickly scanning any paperwork which they might be holding and which is visible, in the hope of gleaning names and addresses. Miss Hall's mistake was to have had the letters in her possession in the first place when briefing political correspondents. Once she blurted out the name Jennifer she should have realised she was on a slippery slope, because even the smallest clue is a start in any journalistic enquiry.

Labour were forced to change their campaign tactics because of the row over the 'Jennifer's ear' broadcast. Instead of opening a new offensive on education they stuck to health, parading their own line-up of sympathetic medical professionals. Labour's thinking was that if they moved off health, as originally planned, it might be misinterpreted as a sign of panic.

However, failures in Labour's procedures for checking hospital case histories were acknowledged by Mr Kinnock. He said there would be no recurrence. After some harsh recriminations, party strategists accepted that they were detracting from their own campaign by indulging in shoddy practices. Mr Patten pounced on the weakness in Labour's position. He said the whole disagreeable mess resulted from trying to make political capital out of cases of personal distress. Mr Major, who claimed Labour's conduct was making the public squirm, stood his ground when asked if Central Office was right to have contacted the *Daily Express*. 'Entirely right,' replied the prime minister.

Neither side wished to get embroiled any further. The priority was to put derailed campaigns back on track. My impression was that Labour had taken the hardest knock. No longer was their election nerve centre running as smoothly as it had been. After establishing what had seemed like unstoppable momentum, Labour tacticians were suddenly unsure of themselves.

For the Conservatives, who by now had endured over two weeks of bad publicity, the Waldegrave fiasco was yet another unfortunate diversion. The shambles of the news conference was regarded as a further salutary reminder of their own complacency in thinking that Mr Patten could run a general election campaign, while at the same time defending his marginal seat. Within Central Office there was a general recognition that Shaun Woodward would have been wiser to have found a strong chairman to back up the health secretary or cancelled that news conference altogether. However, instructions were already issued for what the Tories considered their really critical change of tack: the refocussing of their tax campaign on average families, not just those with higher incomes.

Mr Major found a neat way to turn the tables at one of his own photo-opportunities, borrowing a trick from Mrs Thatcher's 1987 campaign. In the process he appeared to give an implicit endorsement of ITN's coverage of the campaign. For his photo-opportunity in reverse, Mr Major held an ITN camera and started filming the camera crews and photographers. The film he shot was included in ITN's evening news coverage, providing them with a useful prime ministerial plug. Mr Major enjoyed his role reversal, ensuring himself at least one moment of light relief in a troubled week.

CHAPTER 5

John Major was about to break free. In one defiant act he cast off all the carefully crafted image building of Central Office and reverted to a political prop of his youth: a soapbox. But the weekend which was to become a personal turning point for the prime minister could hardly have begun more inauspiciously.

Friday evening's news bulletins gave prominence to a demand by Mrs Thatcher for the Tory party to start addressing the 'big issues.' Her insistence that the campaign had to get back to basics was applauded in an editorial in the ultra-loyal *Daily Mail*. It thanked 'the lady, God bless her' for having thrown 'a typically well directed bucket of cold water' over the raucous row surrounding Labour's 'Jennifer's ear' broadcast. Urging the Tories to get back to the key issues of the economy, defence and Europe, Mr Major and his government were advised by the *Daily Mail* to start putting their case with force and clarity. 'If they do not do so, then they will lose. And they will deserve to lose.'

This trenchant broadside was provoked partly by what the paper's editor Sir David English considered an unwarranted snub. He was angry that Central Office had tipped off the *Daily Express*, rather than the *Daily Mail*, about the telephone call from the hospital consultant responsible for Jennifer Bennett's case.

When an authoritative Tory mouthpiece like the *Daily Mail* is prepared to speculate openly on the prospect of defeat, the rest of the news media need no further encouragement. The command went out from every newsroom: round up the 'usual suspects.' All political parties have MPs and senior figures who find it hard to hold back when invited to comment by newspapers or asked to give interviews for television and radio.

Labour's stage army was firmly back in barracks: nothing, it seemed, was going to tempt left wing critics of Neil Kinnock to put their heads above the parapet. However, there were persistent signs that pent up frustration in the Tory party was reaching boiling point. The pressure was relieved a little at the Thatcher–Major reconciliation the previous Sunday, but the chaotic scenes at William Waldegrave's news conference rubbed in the inadequacies of the Conservatives' election tactics. Before Mr Major could display his own dogged determination and strike free from his media minders, he had to reign back the growing grassroots dissent.

One of the first to break ranks was Geoffrey Dickens, speaking from his consitituency of Littleborough and Saddleworth. He was openly critical of a less than 'sparkling' campaign. Two retiring MPs gave their views on *Today*. Sir Robert McCrindle thought the election had reached a pivotal weekend. He urged Mr Major to take the initiative. The former party chairman, Cecil Parkinson, said the Conservatives had allowed themselves to be distracted. He believed party strategists had not played Mr Major in the right perspective. 'I don't think he's coming over as half the person that he really is.'

The readiness of two elder statesmen to voice publicly what many in the party had been saying privately, had an unsettling effect on the morning news conference. Michael Heseltine refused to respond to the comments of 'armchair experts.' However, I thought he seemed distinctly edgy. Sir Robin Day succeeded where other questioners failed: he enticed the environment secretary away from his prepared answers. Sir Robin quoted the morning's editorial in *The Times* which described how the gulf between the 'leaden spokesmanship of most members of the cabinet and the Archie Rice performances of Michael Heseltine' had become embarrassing.

Clearly flattered by Sir Robin's comparison of him with the fictional music hall comedian from John Osborne's *The Entertainer*, Mr Heseltine was a little more revealing than perhaps he intended: 'I suppose I have been in the cabinet rather less time than most of them, and therefore have suffered less under the weight of high office. I am by nature a backbencher.' Realising the implication of this remark the home secretary, Kenneth Baker, who was sharing the platform, interjected to say that their campaign would make sure Mr Heseltine's backbench career was 'not resumed.' Mr Heseltine remained somewhat agitated. When challenged a little later about the Conservatives' apparent 'hyper wobble' he launched into a lengthy exposition on the failure of the news media to allow politicians to 'talk about our policies and to put forward our positive ideas.' He insisted that the parties wanted to get back to the issues. 'I do beg of the news media to give us the chance to stay on the issues. We depend on you.'

The assertion that the Conservatives were somehow being prevented by journalists from putting across their positive ideas was a bit rich when we were all busily reporting a succession of complaints from within the party that the Tory campaign was too negative. The previous evening, far from sounding constructive, Mr Heseltine excelled himself in a tour-de-force of anti-Labour knockabout based on the musical Oliver. In his imaginary cast list Mr Kinnock played the Artful Dodger and John Smith was Fagin. Mr Heseltine sang his own ditty: 'Can't you just hear the song he hums to himself as he studies Labour's spending plans? "How do I pay the bills? How do I finance these promises?" Fagin knew. John Smith knows. Large sums of money don't grow on trees. You gotta pick a pocket or two."'

I was reminded of Mr Heseltine's performance and some of Dickens' more mournful characters on seeing a downcast huddle in the corner. Maurice Saatchi was in the middle gazing sorrowfully across at the billboards where his agency's posters had previously been displayed. Gone were all the red L-plate signs. All that remained was one stark, solitary slogan: 'Towards 2000.'

Lacking the embellishment of the blue and red Tory torch, it had only one point to commend it: at last the Conservatives had found a positive message. The theme of the morning was UK 2000, a new inner cities initiative from Mr Heseltine, together with details from Mr Baker of the Conservatives' plan for a Millennium Fund. But no wonder Mr Saatchi looked so distressed. The slogan was so devoid of impact it was enough to make an advertising man weep.

My questions failed to elicit an explanation for the removal of Mr Saatchi's cherished posters. When asked if they were considered too negative, the platform party gave knowing, but non-committal, smiles. At Friday's news conference, damp patches were still visible coming through the plain backing paper covering up the remnants of one of Saatchi's more fearsome displays. Under the heading 'Five Years Hard Labour' the poster depicted a woman chained to three balls carrying the messages 'taxes up, mortgages up, prices up.' There was to be no respite for the Conservatives. *The World At One* had lined up more senior Tories eager to pronounce on the campaign. Kenneth Warren, a senior Conservative, said their words needed sharpening, their image improving. 'I would like to see Kenneth Clarke and David Mellor having a hair cut and Mr Heseltine wearing glasses that fit.' Sir Marcus Fox, Conservative MP for Shipley, implored the party to be more forceful. 'We are going to have to change tack. Let's get away from this defensive attitude.'

For a moment the knives came out for Shaun Woodward, who had invested so much of his authority in the informality of the 'Meet John Major' sessions and the showbiz glitz of the roadshow rallies. Sir Marcus was not impressed: 'The way they planned to present him has not come off. On the doorstep everyone likes John Major. He is such a nice man. I know he has strength when he is riled by Labour. He needs to show that fighting spirit.'

Out on the campaign trail, in Welwyn Garden City, Mr Major brushed aside a reporter's question about jitters in the party. He insisted the Conservatives were going to win. However, minutes later David Evans, the candidate being supported by Mr Major,

MAJOR

Bullet-proof glass protected John Major in his campaign coach which was also reinforced with armour-plating. A terrorist attack was a constant threat. 'Don't you realise the IRA are trying to kill one of us?' said Chris Patten early in the campaign.

Neil Kinnock's walkabouts were few. On those occasions when he was photographed on the move the aim was to make him look as prime ministerial as possible.

Intimate question-and-answer sessions were conceived as a way of portraying the real John Major. Conservative supporters in his Huntingdon constituency were invited to the first of his fireside chats (15 March). BBC correspondent John Simpson described the format as 'desperately tame', sparking off Tory protests.

John Major was ready to take on left-wing protestors at Luton (22 March). After being jostled in Bolton the previous week he had a soapbox and loud-hailer carried on his campaign coach. The Prime Minister found street-corner oratory reminded him of his teenage soapbox speeches in Brixton market.

Left: The slogan 'My vote' on Paddy Ashdown's podium reinforced the message that support for the Liberal Democrats was not a wasted vote. Neil Kinnock's opening line at Labour's rally in Sheffield (1 April) was: 'We're all right.' His chant was repeated by the audience. An artificial wind machine kept the flags fluttering above Mr Kinnock's head. The set for John Major's roadshow was designed by Andrew Lloyd Webber and reputedly cost £500,000.

Julie Hall, press secretary to Neil Kinnock, found herself at the centre of the controversy which developed over the leaking of Jennifer Bennett's name (see below).

A Labour party election broadcast showed a young girl with excruciating earache who had to wait nine months for an operation. But a protest over hospital waiting lists got lost amid argument over who revealed the child's name.

Paddy Ashdown was fretful at first about the shiny steel framework erected on his news conference platform. Was it really 'modern and urgent'? Mr Ashdown paid tribute to the work of Des Wilson, saying he could not have coped without his support as campaign director.

Paddy Ashdown enjoying a warm-up chat with Jonathan Dimbleby, host of television's *Election Call*. Journalists and television crews considered Mr Ashdown the most media-friendly of the party leaders.

An egg thrown during a walk-about near Southampton (6 April) threw John Major off balance and cut his face.

Labour claimed 'desperate smear tactics' by tabloid newspapers were one reason for their failure to win many of the marginal constituencies. *The Sun*'s two final front pages were described by Conservatives as 'brilliant examples of popular journalism'. Des Wilson considered particularly effective the Conservatives' portrayal of the Liberal Democrats as the Trojan horse for an unelectable Labour party.

Shaun Woodward, the Conservatives' director of communications, played a key role in their campaign. Formerly editor of *That's Life*, he drew on his experience as a BBC television producer to devise ways of portraying John Major as a man of the people.

Seven thousand billboard sites were used to display posters prepared for the Conservatives by Saatchi and Saatchi. The posters also formed a backdrop to news conferences. Chris Patten usually chaired the proceedings and is seen here fielding questions with Michael Heseltine and Michael Howard.

His own mandate at last! Election victory was all the sweeter for John Major because he confounded opinion pollsters and pundits. Within a few hours of waving to supporters outside Central Office, he had the news media dancing to his tune as they awaited his victory speech in Downing Street.

became vitriolic. 'The failure is the people running the campaign from Central Office. It's as simple as that. You know who they are. You don't need me to be specific. I have an adjective for them but I won't use it.'

Mr Major intended delivering his verdict on the Tory media strategists not in words but action. Ever since he was jostled in Bolton by what he considered to be a left wing rent-a-mob, he had been thinking about ways to respond if future walk-abouts were disrupted. He was determined he would not be prevented by demonstrators from communicating with Conservative supporters. I knew from conversations with members of his campaign team that the demonstration had affected him profoundly. For the first time in 16 months as prime minister he had been caught in the middle of a hostile crowd. Two days later Peter MacMahon of the *Sunday Mirror* had remonstrated with him for complaining about this. As Mr MacMahon pointed out, such protestations sounded pathetic coming from a politician who started out on a soapbox in Brixton.

After Welwyn and Hatfield the next stop for Mr Major's campaign bus was Luton. A stout wooden document box was tucked away in the luggage compartment of the armour plated coach. Luton was about to become a political landmark.

As Mr Major arrived in the shopping centre, demonstrators were lying in wait. Many were carrying banners of the Socialist Workers party. Police officers struggled to form a cordon around Mr Major. Minders dragged out the soapbox. Gripping a loud-hailer, Mr Major was ready at last to be himself: 'Can you hear? Don't let the people who take to the streets take your vote away. How do you expect people in the world to listen to a socialist prime minister when all over the world, the world is ticking socialism off. This is not the sort of country that will put the mobs back on the streets like before in 1979.'

Old fashioned street corner campaigning was like a tonic, wiping away the memory of all those wounding remarks about lacklustre speeches and Dalek-like delivery. As the hecklers tried to drown out the cheers of his supporters, Mr Major was spurred on to display the kind of political opportunism that had taken him to Number 10. A child in the crowd was suddenly up with the prime minister on his soapbox: 'This is the boy the future's about. This is what the election's about . . . this boy's future.'

Mr Major's soapbox confrontation led television news bulletins all day. Neil Kinnock was also featured in an unexpected photo-opportunity for which, in his case, he had the news media to thank. Journalists, photographers and television cameramen, all wearing red T-shirts emblazoned with the figure 50, were lined up in a birthday celebration as he arrived at Prestwick. 'Brilliant, marvellous,' said Mr Kinnock as the assembled company started singing *Happy Birthday*.

Labour were keen to make the most of the Tory infighting. Mr Kinnock commiserated. 'They've obviously got some difficulties on the bridge. In fact, as far as I can see, the bridge may be deserted.' Bryan Gould went for the ship's captain: 'We are told that the latest decision is to play to the strengths of John Major. We understand a working party has now been set up to discover what they are.' Just as Labour were pushed to the sidelines by Mr Major's transformation, so were the Liberal Democrats. They approached the end of the week feeling rather aggrieved. Throughout the row over Labour's 'Jennifer's ear' broadcast, Paddy Ashdown refused to enter the two party dogfight. Opponents saw this as vote losing piety but he was convinced that the avoidance of negative tactics was striking a chord with the public.

One consequence of Mr Ashdown's principled stand was that the Liberal Democrats lost out on what they considered to be their rightful share of television coverage. Des Wilson complained to the BBC and the Independent Television Commission. In the first three days of the week their share on BBC was 18.5% and 23% of ITN. Because the Liberal Democrats believed their allocation should be 28.5%, Mr Wilson said he was taking legal advice. Broadcasters rejected the complaints, saying that the primary consideration was news value. A stopwatch was only one factor for calculating fair coverage.

The Liberal Democrats had taken a risk by building their campaign so firmly around the personality of Mr Ashdown. There were some murmurings of disquiet. Lady Seear, a former leader of the Liberal peers, was interviewed campaigning in Chesterfield by *The World At One*. She seemed to be missing out on the action, miffed at not appearing on the platform of the London news conferences as in previous elections. 'This time they are using the leader, and sending us round the country.' When asked whether the concentration on Mr Ashdown would work, Lady Seear replied: 'We shall see.'

After their Saturday morning news conference Mr Wilson dispelled any doubts. He seemed to me as ebullient as ever, having shaken off his annoyance with the broadcasters. 'I am convinced we have had the best week so far. We stuck to our battle plan, our high risk strategy of going on education and an extra penny on income tax, and it has paid off.'

Mr Wilson had good grounds for optimism. Five opinion polls for Sunday newspapers showed an improvement in the Liberal Democrats' rating. The BBC's poll of polls confirmed that

Mr Ashdown was the real gainer of the week, his party having climbed a full four points since the election was called. With less than half the campaign to go, party strategists waited nervously for the weekend opinion polls. The percentages averaged: Labour 39%, Conservative 37%, Liberal Democrats 19%.

SUNDAY 29 MARCH DAY 19

Buoyed up by their improved opinion poll ratings, the Liberal Democrats set sail for the most inspired media sortie of the election: Paddy's day trip to Boulogne. It was the first known example of a party leader taking his campaign abroad. Mr Ashdown was determined to highlight what he thought was a forgotten issue in the campaign, the need for decisive steps towards European monetary and political union. Fifty children on a school trip from Edinburgh waved flags as Mr Ashdown arrived for his sea front meeting with French and Belgian Liberal Democrats. He spoke first in French, then in English. Reporters found him in good humour. His tetchiness about being marginalised in the Jennifer Bennett row had evaporated. Mr Ashdown would not be drawn on the Liberal Democrats' surge in the opinion polls. 'We are a mature party that doesn't go bonkers over such things.'

John Major, who was staying at Chequers, started celebrations for his 49th birthday by taking Norma to the Mothering Sunday service. On leaving church he told reporters: 'No politics, it's Sunday.' Later he set off for Central Office where staff donned T-shirts bearing the logo 'JM-49' and he cut a birthday cake, iced in blue and white, bearing a rosette reading 'JM 4 PM.' Once the party was over Mr Major had an important engagement: a lobby briefing which never officially took place. Upstairs in the chairman's office, where the walls are lined with photographs of Mr Patten's wife and daughters, the prime minister met a select group of political editors known as the 'White Commonwealth.' The origin and title of the group goes back nearly 30 years, to the days of tense Commonwealth conflict, when Harold Wilson was prime minister. He built up a clique of political editors who were known to be sympathetic and whom he felt he could trust. They were invited to special briefings in Downing Street.

The membership and political complexion of Mr Major's 'White Commonwealth' owed much to the Thatcher years when her government cemented particularly close ties with Fleet Street. The journalists seen climbing the stairs to Mr Patten's office were representatives of *The Times,* the *Daily Telegraph,* the *Daily Mail,* the *Daily Express, The Sun* and the *Daily Star.* There were no political editors or correspondents from broadcasting organisations or from those newspapers critical of the government. To have invited their representatives would have been too risky. Mr Major knew that he could rely on the representatives of those six newspapers to keep the discussions secret. Broadcasters, and journalists from other newspapers, would have felt compromised and tempted to reveal the source of their information.

Because Mr Major knew he was among friends he was anxious for feedback. What did the political editors think of his soapbox speech? The general concensus was that it had been a success. Mr Major looked relieved, as though he had been waiting anxiously for independent reaction. He was advised to go on speaking with the same passion and conviction. Mr Major vowed there and then that he would get on his soapbox again and tell the British people what he thought. His soapbox would travel with him for the rest of the campaign.

As the conversation developed Mr Major expanded on his likely tactics. He intended to attack Neil Kinnock in his next speech. The political editors were struck by Mr Major's evident strength of feeling. He said Britain would be dreadful under Mr Kinnock. In an instant one of the journalists could see a headline.

There had been write-ups over the weekend previewing the 1984 cult horror movie *A Nightmare on Elm Street*, about to be reshown on Channel 4. The journalist volunteered a slight variation: 'A Nightmare on Kinnock Street.' Mr Major repeated it to himself once, then twice, savouring the words. There were profuse thanks. He appeared delighted by the suggestion.

Mr Major's decision to call in friendly political editors reflected his anxiety over the way the usually loyal Tory newspapers were behaving. In Mrs Thatcher's day a meeting of the 'White Commonwealth' would have been superfluous. She delegated much of her press liaison work to two long standing advisers, Sir Gordon Reece and Sir Tim Bell. During election campaigns they ensured that Conservative leaning newspapers did not highlight damaging stories about Mrs Thatcher, or her party. They promoted a favourable line on the day's stories when meeting senior political and editorial staff of the *Daily Mail*, the *Daily Express* and *The Sun* for an evening's whisky and chat.

Shaun Woodward was from a younger generation. He came from television, not Fleet Street, and therefore I felt he was inevitably handicapped by his lack of experitse in manipulating that blurred but powerful relationship which has given the Conservative party so much influence over the majority of mass circulation newspapers. So inadequate was the liaison, I was told that Kelvin MacKenzie, the editor of *The Sun*, was among those inquiring about a lack of contact.

One former Thatcher aide, David Hart, chairman of the Committee For a Free Britain, explained to me the reason for their anxiety in the first two weeks of the campaign. 'The tabloid editors are mystified. No one is talking to them or taking an interest in what they are doing. Under Tim Bell and Gordon Reece we could all offer ideas and help work out a strategy. They used to ring round at elections making sure editors knew the line.'

I felt Mr Major probably did not realise that his preference for a freer regime within the party had loosened the tight discipline which Mrs Thatcher previously exercised over Tory newspaper editors. As the campaign progressed I was conscious of changing attitudes among a number of the political correspondents. Some of the journalists whose newspapers always supported the Conservatives seemed to be longing for a greater degree of independence. Others were conscious that their anti-Labour coverage was indefensible and they wished to restore their personal credibility, in case Mr Kinnock won.

DAY **20** MONDAY 30 MARCH

WEEK 4 – 10 DAYS TO GO

Labour and the Conservatives opened the last full week of their campaigns by concentrating on taxation. John Smith repeated that eight out of ten families would gain from Labour's fairer system of tax and national insurance. He presented statistics showing the impact on ten typical families. The two who would lose were a bank manager and his wife in Cambridge and a journalist living in Tonbridge who was married to a public relations executive. Eight other familes with incomes ranging from £6000 to £43 000 a year would all gain.

At Central Office the Conservatives' presentation was more dramatic. On arrival we were all handed leaflets entitled 'Labour's tax bombshell' which claimed a Labour government would cost the average taxpayer an extra £1250 a year. Campaign literature was targeted at skilled workers. All the examples stressed the concentration on the C2 vote: a car assembly worker earning £12 000 would lose £359 a year under Labour; an electrician earning £13 500 would be £503 worse off; and a crane driver on £17 500 would lose £960.

Mr Major reflected his new found confidence with a pledge to continue to widen the scope of the new, lower tax rate of 20 pence in the pound. 'That's the way we mean to go on. Taking more and more taxpayers out of 25 pence tax by widening the band. This way, we can make progress . . . year by year . . . towards a 20 pence basic rate for all.'

When answering questions Mr Major made a point of looking towards the future. He insisted he would try, but could not promise, to widen the 20 pence tax band every year. Chris Patten avoided any gratuitous remarks. After unnecessarily antagonising reporters at previous news conferences, I felt the chairman was definitely attempting to portray a cooler, more restrained image. Sir Norman Fowler, one of Mr Major's campaign advisers, who was on hand to brief journalists, reinforced the line that the Tory campaign would now be steadier for the final push towards polling day. 'We crowded in too much in the early stages. But John's campaign is getting sharper and you will find his speeches will be stronger.'

Patrick Rock, Mr Patten's special adviser, also thought their campaign was settling down. He was pleased that Labour had not gained in the polls from their health broadcast. 'Health was Labour's ace but it's turned into a two of clubs. Our strongest cards are the economy and tax and we haven't really played them yet.' As a parting shot I suggested to him that Mr Patten had been well advised to cease baiting journalists. Mr Rock paused for a moment, thanked me, but refrained from commenting. My observation seemed to have struck a raw nerve.

True to his word the prime minister was out on his soapbox at the first opportunity. Three hundred local Tories gathered as the campaign bus arrived in Cheltenham. Party workers carried out the wooden box and a loud hailer. Mr Major's target was the Liberal Democrats, the main challengers in the constituency. He teased his opponents: 'Can anybody name more than two Liberal spokesmen? There's a prize for three.'

After Luton this was a relatively sedate affair. One heckler shouted 'rubbish' when Mr Major repeated the claim that the average taxpayer would pay £1250 extra a year under Labour. He replied that it was Labour's policies which were rubbish.

In his speech that evening in Birmingham, Mr Major delivered his expected attack on Neil Kinnock. He described the Labour leader as a 'nodding, grinning foot-in-the-door salesman' who had not got the experience to negotiate for Britain. A Labour government would clobber economic recovery, chase away investment, destroy jobs, and bring back flying pickets. 'In other words, A Nightmare on Kinnock Street.'

To make sure television and radio newsrooms had sufficient advance warning of the Kinnock attack, the relevant quotes from the speech were being issued to journalists soon after 5 pm. The aim was to secure the greatest possible news coverage. Because of Mr Major's meeting with political editors from the leading Tory newspapers, I felt that the last had probably not been heard about the prime minister's nightmare vision.

Throughout the day Labour seemed somewhat uncoordinated in their response to the switch which the Conservatives were making over tax. John Smith and the shadow treasury team kept repeating that eight out of ten families would be better off. But the whole emphasis of the Tory counter attack, that the average taxpayer would be £1250 a year worse off under Labour, had been retargeted at skilled workers, the very people whom Mr Smith said would gain from his shadow budget.

I felt that Mr Kinnock sensed the danger and perhaps doubted that enough was being done to refute the Tory figures. At his morning news conference he was asked by Peter Allen, a political correspondent with ITN, to respond to the Conservatives' assertion that Labour's tax plans would devastate the housing market. Mr Kinnock insisted that would not happen. House purchases, he said, were driven by first time buyers and such people would gain under Labour.

On his way out of the news conference Mr Kinnock tried without success to find Mr Allen. He was clearly concerned by the implica- tion of the question, anxious to prevent such allegations gaining currency among broadcasters. Mr Allen was surprised by the trouble Mr Kinnock went to. 'He was asking for me by name. When I got back to the office I was rung by Hilary Coffman from his press office. They were soon faxing me statements. Obviously Mr Kinnock was very worried by what the Tories were saying on tax.'

Mr Kinnock's anxiety resurfaced during his morning tour of West Midlands' marginals when he was questioned about the impact of Labour's tax plans on car workers. Again Mr Kinnock denied that families of skilled workers would lose: 'It's absolute rubbish – unless the average car worker is on £40 or £50 000 a year, and I don't think they are. Everybody earning under £23 000 a year will be better off under our tax proposals.'

Mr Kinnock faced a punishing schedule. After chairing the party news conference in London at 7.45 am and spending the day touring the West Midlands, he was interviewed by David Dimbleby for *Panorama*. The big set-piece interviews are always considered an ordeal. Party managers fear the leader might make a gaffe or be tripped up during questioning. With just over a week to go, Labour strategists were on tenterhooks, dreading the possibility of a last minute mistake. But there was no need for concern. Mr Kinnock was relaxed and confident. The *Panorama* interview passed off without any untoward occurrence, as had his appearance on *Walden* the day before.

DAY **21** TUESDAY 31 MARCH

Conflict over tax continued to preoccupy the politicians. *The Independent* provoked considerable discussion by publishing a report prepared by city accountants Coopers and Lybrand Deloitte, which showed that higher taxes would be needed if *either* party were elected, when they sought to implement their spending plans. The report showed that Labour would have to raise the basic rate of income tax by the equivalent of 5 pence and the Conservatives by 4 pence.

Neil Kinnock shrugged off the report. Any suggestion that Labour's spending plans could possibly total £27 billion relied on 'crystal ball gazing' rather than proper examination of their policies and commitments. John Major was equally adamant that the spending figures suggested for the government were inaccurate. He repeated his pledge that in the next parliament the Conservatives would reduce direct taxation. If an annual cut of a penny was not possible Mr Major undertook at least to widen the scope of the 20 pence tax band every year.

A front page report in the *Daily Mail*, billed as exclusive, revealed a secret Labour document stating that public sector employees would receive annual pay increases worth 1% more than the private sector norm. This was described as a remarkable 'sweetheart' deal which Labour had reached with their union paymasters. The original document was dated January 1990 and copies of it were handed out by the Conservatives. An accompanying statement by Norman Lamont said it was the final proof that Labour would 'spend, spend,

spend.' Reporters on the other Tory tabloids told me that the leaked document had been given to the *Daily Mail* by Central Office in an attempt to make amends for tipping off the *Daily Express* in the Jennifer Bennett case.

An exclusive was also claimed by *The Sun* which led its front page with the headline: 'Benn: We'll Turn Red in Number 10.' The basis for this was a Channel 4 interview in which Tony Benn said he hoped the link between the next Labour government and the unions would be 'at least as strong as the link between the Conservatives and big business.' Although Mr Benn's remark hardly supported the headline, I knew that any comment about Labour's link with the unions was potentially newsworthy, especially if delivered during the campaign. However, on checking with Channel 4, I was told that the interview was recorded at the end of January.

The Sun's report was under the byline of Simon Walters, a political correspondent. He told me that the trouble with the campaign for the tabloids was that there had been no big arguments, except for the row over Jennifer's ear. 'Everyone knows the Conservatives can't afford large tax cuts and that Labour won't be able to spend much more. So all this election stuff is phony and everyone knew it would be.'

Trade union leaders were noticeably absent from the campaign. In fact there were very few sightings of the small group of union leaders who were known to be advising Mr Kinnock. On the day the manifesto was approved I did see John Edmonds, the GMB general secretary, who was a member of a committee of inner advisers. I also met Bill Morris, general secretary of the Transport and General Workers. Mr Morris was excited by Labour's continued lead in the opinion polls. However, he was anxious about the impact Mr Major was creating by speaking from his soapbox. 'Major really is coming over much stronger. Before, he looked frightened of meeting people when he was in those staged question sessions. He's certainly not frit anymore.'

Although union leaders themselves were holding back, they were providing invaluable assistance to Labour in addition to the money which they contributed to the election fighting fund. Most of the unions seconded their own press officers to assist David Hill's communications department. Phil Woolas of the GMB was among those who played a leading role. Help was also being provided by the Amalgamated Engineering Union, the National Union of Public Employees and the National Communications Union.

The value of these press officers to Labour's publicity machine lay partly in their detailed knowledge of the sensitive issues which should be avoided, in order to prevent embarrassing stories about Labour's link with the unions. Mr Woolas thought their contribution was significant: 'The unions have had 13 years in the trenches under Thatcher, so we've had plenty of time to get our press and communications teams into shape. I think we are more experienced than the Conservatives in avoiding trouble.'

There was no doubt that Mr Woolas had a point, and I was surprised by how few of the Conservatives' regular scare stories seemed to have any lasting impact. An example of the failure to create a stir was the lukewarm response to a claim that many Labour candidates had hidden their links with the Campaign for Nuclear Disarmament. On arriving at Central Office we were handed reprints of 'before' and 'after' documents showing how all reference to CND membership had been expunged. Great play was made of a dossier containing biographical details which had allegedly been doctored. Some reporters thought Labour had acted pretty shamelessly, but said they would not have expected anything else because of the fuss the Conservatives made over nuclear weapons. It struck me that any candidate of whatever persuasion was naturally going to put the best possible gloss on biographies prepared by their parties.

The news conference was intended as a trailer for the Conservatives' election broadcast later in the evening which described the 'CND cover-up' and asked whether the country could trust Mr Kinnock on defence. Michael Heseltine repeated the charge in a speech, claiming defence strategy could not be learned in the 'nurseries of CND.' He ridiculed claims that Mr Kinnock could be trusted: 'It's the biggest load of Kinnocks I have ever heard.'

On the way into Central Office I was handed a photostat of the front page of the *Bath Evening Chronicle*. Copies were being handed out by jubiliant Liberal Democrats. They were pointing excitedly to the lead story. It said that a local opinion poll was indicating that Mr Patten would lose his seat.

Later, as a group of reporters gathered round Mr Patten and we started chatting, I thought he looked fed up, as if he could not take much more. He valiantly threw back at us our opening jibes about what might happen to him in Bath. He seemed in a reflective mood, ready to discuss the campaign. He thought journalists had a lot to answer for because of the way we allowed the opinion polls to set the news agenda. He had clearly been stung by criticism from within the party.

'Yes, you could say we felt pretty pissed off at the weekend when we had all that guff about our campaign wobbling. It was the usual retired colonel brigade and a few people who used to work here. Their views are as irrelevant now as they were then.' When we pressed him about the opinion polls, Mr Patten remained confident that the Conservatives would win. 'We know our tax campaign won't hit home until the last week. What we've got to do is turn out our firm vote of 40% to 42%. That's enough to win. And, don't forget the incumbency factor. Our MPs in the marginals have seen a lot of old ladies. That'll help on polling day.'

There was hardly time to reflect on what Mr Patten had said before news started coming through of three new opinion polls, each putting Labour in front. The Labour leads were four, six and seven points. The seven point lead was the largest Labour had achieved in any opinion poll for four months. Labour predicted all day that they would be ahead, but the party did not expect the margin to be so great.

Mr Kinnock was delighted, confident of substantial gains and a majority Labour government. Jack Cunningham agreed to appear on television and radio. However, he wanted to record only one joint interview, reporters being limited to one question each. I knew there was no point in protesting. Labour had the upper hand and could dictate terms.

Back at Central Office there were long, drawn faces. We had to wait some time for Mr Patten to appear. He insisted on doing his interviews separately and as each one was conducted all the other camera crews and reporters had to leave the room. My radio interview was last. By the time I got to Mr Patten, he looked whacked. He was slumped in a chair. I realised this was a moment to go gently. Mr Patten's press officer, Angie Bray, was her usual cheerful self. 'Look, Chris had his hair cut today. Doesn't it look better?' By now the chairman's answer was word perfect: 'If the polls are correct, then there are some people who usually vote Conservative who think they can make a safe protest by voting Liberal. We must remind them that if they do that they will get a Labour government.'

Waiting for the interviews to finish was the chief whip Richard Ryder. He looked harassed and nothing like as cheerful as he had the week before. He insisted he would not comment. 'Whatever Chris has said about the opinion polls is also my view.' Mr Ryder was equally determined not to appear rattled. 'I love elections. I adore them.' As the tension eased a little he told me it was a night for cool nerves. 'Later on I shall take Chris out for dinner and cheer him up.'

As I left Central Office I could not help thinking that this must be what it was like on the bridge of a supertanker, drifting in a storm without an engine or steering: and the chief mate had just told the captain that there was nothing for it but to have a drink and sit it out.

WEDNESDAY I APRIL

Even the most cautious among Labour's strategists and advisers were unable to quell the exhilaration gripping their campaign team. The party's belief in the impetus for change seemed about to be vindicated. No one could remember a day when the morning newspapers were such a joy to behold. Splashed across the front page of *The Times* was the bold headline: 'Poll gives Labour seven point lead.' Exactly a week after lambasting the party for a 'sick NHS stunt' the *Daily Express* led on Labour's opinion poll hat trick, reporting that with Neil Kinnock on course for Downing Street the 'alarm bells are now ringing at Tory Central Office.'

At Labour's media headquarters in Millbank there appeared every justification for confidence. Leads of four, six and seven points, reported in the three latest opinion polls, were higher than expected, but were all well in line with local and regional surveys being conducted in marginal constituencies. All around the signs were positive, as if a sense of momentum was being generated by their slogan: 'It's time for a change. It's time for Labour.'

The party leadership was sustained throughout the opening weeks of the campaign by the conviction that Labour's policy proposals were virtually foolproof. They had been worked at over and over again to iron out all possible pitfalls. Admittedly there was the problem of the relaunch of the Conservatives' 'tax bombshell' scare, but that was regarded as troublesome rather than fatal. After all Labour fought back successfully in January when the Tories last attacked them on tax, and they were fighting back again. Great faith was placed in opinion poll data showing that voters favoured increased public spending rather than tax cuts.

In the Labour communications department all talk focussed on the mass rally in Sheffield that evening. I had not realised the scale of the extravaganza Labour were planning. Ten thousand people were expected to attend what was billed as the biggest political rally of the decade. There would be a complete evening's entertainment: pop music and soul, opera and a brass band, endorsements by pop stars, actors and athletes as well as a speech by Neil Kinnock.

Gerard Sagar, the chief press and broadcasting officer, described how five television cameras would film the event so that live coverage could be beamed up to the Starbird satellite. 'We are getting tremendous interest from abroad. The rally and Neil's speech will be available free and live to television stations across America, Europe and Russia.'

David Hill, the director of communications, was just as enthusiastic about the rally and the impact it might have. Unlike the rest of his team he experienced a taste of power when Labour were last in office. His long years of service as a political adviser included a period in the late 1970s when Roy Hattersley was secretary of state for prices and consumer protection. I never heard Mr Hill tempt fate by speculating about his own political future, but I knew he would be well placed if Labour won. He always smiled when teased by journalists about the likelihood of becoming the next Downing Street press secretary. Nevertheless, as he gave me his assessment of the opinion polls, I sensed a tangible longing for government which echoed throughout the Labour movement.

'Obviously we didn't expect the polls to give us quite the lead they have. But we are exactly where we wanted to be for our mega-rally tonight. It'll be the launch pad for our final week. We have kept our nerve, stuck rigidly to our strategy and we are ahead.'

Mr Hill acknowledged that a few things had gone wrong: they

were forced to change tack because of the row over the 'Jennifer's ear' health broadcast but, compared with the violent swings in the Conservatives' campaign tactics, he felt that their change of tack was minor. 'They spent 15 months grooming Major and look what they do with him: put him on a soapbox and give him a loud hailer. It looks as if he's touting for votes, imploring people to back him. It's an amazing mistake. He has unsettled his own supporters. Nothing has assisted us more. It makes Neil Kinnock look like prime minister.'

At his morning news conference, reflecting that upbeat assessment, Mr Kinnock told a questioner that, apart from a slight cough, he thought his fitness to govern was 'damn near perfect.' His private advice to the campaign team was that of a rugby captain: don't make loose mistakes, keep tight-bound and shove. But he could not have appeared more confident: his team was winning. All they needed to do was hang on to their lead.

At his news conference the prime minister followed up Chris Patten's warning to Conservative waverers. Mr Major said there was no soft option: 'If the opinion polls are right, Labour's support has remained precisely where it was. What we have seen is a portion of Conservative support apparently moving to the Liberal party. Now that makes crystal clear a point we have stated repeatedly. Unless people vote directly for Conservative candidates they will end up with a Labour government.'

The Conservatives' all-out assault on the Liberal Democrats was the most dramatic switch of all in their tactics: a violent and unexpected push to stop support slipping away. Before, the Tories were content to snipe away at Liberal Democrat candidates in those constituencies where they represented a threat, but otherwise they ignored or ridiculed them. Some strengthening in Paddy Ashdown's position was welcomed by the Conservatives because it split the opposition vote, but the polls were now showing that the Liberal Democrats' surge was getting too close for comfort. Mr Ashdown's response to this hurried manoeuvring was to accuse the government of being in terminal retreat, not knowing which way to turn. 'I don't care how they insult us. I don't care how they try to scare people into the ballot box. We are not changing our strategy.'

Mr Major spent most of the day in the West Country, the front line of his second front, where the Liberal Democrats were busily targeting many Tory seats. Speaking from his soapbox at Thornbury, near Bristol, Mr Major warned of the dangers to Britain if it returned to the Lib–Lab pact of the late 1970s. He struck out at Liberal Democrats in the crowd: 'There they are, the Trojan horse, the people who let in a Labour government in 1974.'

Hecklers were welcomed, especially one man who suggested that the government should do more to build up the NHS. Mr Major was in his element: 'Who is he, this Rip Van Winkle, that he has not seen what's been happening? How many new hospitals has he not seen being built in this country, how many new patients has he not seen being treated in this country?'

The sight of a prime minister campaigning from a soapbox became quite a talking point. Questions were asked regularly at his news conferences. Mr Major insisted he was enjoying it. 'Perhaps we should have started using it earlier. I don't know. But wherever I go from now on in the campaign I shall take that soapbox with me.'

Despite Mr Major's faith in street corner oratory, doubts were expressed within the party. Edwina Currie echoed David Hill's point that there was a danger of Mr Major looking like the leader of the opposition. 'It's lovely to see John on a soapbox out on the stump. But Neil Kinnock is moving around in a Daimler. It's very clever stuff. I am surprised our campaign managers have done nothing about it.'

Anxiety was also creeping in to the offices of Conservative-supporting newspapers. One political editor described how the executives at his paper held their heads in amazement every time Mr Major popped up on his soapbox. Another correspondent said one group of Tory advisers were suggesting that Mr Major should give it up. Others were warning that if the soapbox was suddenly abandoned this would, of itself, create a damaging news story. Mr Major remained unmoved by the criticism. The comparison which struck me most was with the 1983 general election when almost every day Michael Foot was shown on television walking his Tibetan terrier Dizzie on Hampstead Heath. The 1992 election was adding a soapbox to the long list of political props.

More worrying for the Conservatives was the gossip among journalists that Mr Major was becoming a lame duck prime minister. The verdict was that the best he could hope for would be to end up with the largest number of seats, not an overall majority. The danger of such talk was that it could influence news coverage and the way reporters approached the day's events.

In an attempt to dispel doubt and generate an air of confidence, key party stalwarts attended important Tory news conferences. Their presence implied stability even though they found it difficult to spread reassurance. After the Conservatives' set back in the opinion polls there was a particularly strong turnout. Sir William Clark, the retiring Conservative MP for Croydon South, who was sitting next to me, insisted they would not be changing tack. He was backed up by Lord Waddington, the retiring leader of the Lords, who assured me that the Tories had quite a few shots left in their locker.

I felt there was probably more to be gleaned by joining reporters in the foyer where *The Independent's* Anthony Bevins was grilling Shaun Woodward. At the very moment the director of communications was asked if he was now the scapegoat for a failed campaign, he was saved by a television crew who were attracted by the confrontation and started filming surreptitiously. Mr Woodward protested at being filmed, but before departing upstairs he acknowledged the pressures of the job: 'You have to take the praise and the flak. I have no quibbles with that.'

The impact of the polls was devastating. Chris Buckland, a *Daily Express* columnist, said Central Office could not understand where Labour's seven point lead had come from. The sense of disbelief was reinforced by Mr Patten's adviser Patrick Rock. 'We are completely taken aback by the latest polls. We don't trust them. What the pollsters are saying just isn't what we are hearing on the doorsteps.'

All afternoon the atmosphere remained tense on Mr Major's campaign coach. His advisers waited anxiously for some hint of the *Daily Telegraph's* latest Gallup poll, due to be published the following morning. At last the call came through. Mr Major was told the result immediately: Gallup was giving the Conservatives a half point lead. Finally there was independent verification of the Conservatives' hunch that Labour's lead was wildly exaggerated. So great was their relief that the campaign team forgot they had been tipped off in advance in the strictest confidence. The news started leaking back to London even before it had been fully circulated within the *Daily Telegraph* itself.

When details of the Gallup poll were released officially, later that evening, Labour's presidential-style rally had already begun. The news flash from the Press Association was timed at 6.38 pm. At 6.52 pm a huge video screen in Sheffield showed pictures of Neil and Glenys Kinnock's arrival. The commentary was delivered in ecstatic terms: 'You'll see Neil Kinnock's helicopter on the screen, landing just a few hundred yards from the arena entrance. Neil has been a busy man, living up to his reputation as one of the greatest political campaigners of all time.'

The fact that Gallup was contradicting the earlier Labour leads was regarded as a blessing in disguise by one member of Labour's media team. Phil Woolas, an ex-BBC journalist, recognised the possibility that Labour might be damaged if the atmosphere in Sheffield became too euphoric. 'I knew there was a danger that this might happen after those six and seven point leads. We had to avoid being complacent. That was why news of Gallup putting the Tories ahead was so important. But it was not until the interval that we could alert the people on stage to the fact that the Gallup poll was against us. We kept saying to everyone in Sheffield: "Steady on, don't appear over confident." '

For journalists like myself watching the live coverage in London, the Sheffield rally was a dazzling spectacle. Desks in the BBC newsroom at Millbank are fitted with small television sets which can receive domestic and satellite channels, as well as incoming television signals from outside broadcasts around the country. John Major and Paddy Ashdown were also giving televised speeches that evening, but nothing could match the pictures from Sheffield.

For the first time a British political party was trying to equal the razzmatazz of an American political convention. The pop music, soul and opera provided something for all ages and tastes. Party endorsements were given by the athlete Steve Cram, actor Stephen Fry, film producer David Puttnam and Mick Hucknall, lead singer of the group Simply Red, who spoke on video from Marseilles.

Neil Kinnock's arrival on stage was reminiscent of a 1960s pop concert. Punching his fists together he delivered his opening line: 'We're all right.' The audience shouted back: 'We're all right.' He and the audience repeated their welcome to each other. High up on one side of the enormous stage were six flags: the Union Jack, the four flags of the United Kingdom and the flag of the European community, fluttering in a breeze created by a wind machine. Beneath them was the podium from which Mr Kinnock was speaking. On the other side of the stage was an enormous video screen which simultaneously relayed Mr Kinnock's speech. Below the screen, sitting in a long row, were the shadow cabinet, their silhouettes picked out by the lighting. Clearly moved by his reception, Mr Kinnock asked if they could ever have imagined the modern Conservative party arranging such a night. 'But this is the Labour party, this is the party that is going to win the election and win for our country.'

Mr Kinnock matched the drama of the occasion with a passionate speech. The country could not re-elect a government which was impoverishing the people who were already poor: the pensioners, the disabled, the unemployed and single parents. These people made up more than a quarter of the poor in the European community. Yet the Tories were breaking an all party concensus of 40 years to reduce the plague of poverty and never increase it.

'You can't go on with deliberate policies of poverty. I don't preach envy. What I draw attention to is the widening chasm between the richest and the poorest. What I call for is justice.'

The applause from the vast audience was powerful and moving. Mr Kinnock captured the moment: 'What's at issue in this election is not the soapboxes that the prime minister stands on, it's the cardboard boxes that people have to live in, that's an issue in this election.' So strong were the emotions released by the speech and its setting that I wanted reaction both from within the Labour party and from their opponents. Mr Kinnock had an unshakeable belief in the power of these events, in the way they could build up morale among party workers. In his years as leader he transformed party conferences. They progressed from being decorated with roses to stages for choreographed performances by the shadow cabinet. The 1991 conference ended with the platform party holding their hands above their heads swaying together to Queen and *We Are the Champions*.

It was difficult to sort out my own feelings and make an assessment. As I expected, Labour's media office were saying the rally was tremendous and would definitely inspire party workers for the final week of the campaign. A correspondent on the *Daily Telegraph* told me they were getting phone calls from retired colonels complaining that the Union Jack was flying upside down above Mr Kinnock's head. Tory Central Office said they were hearing protests from pensioners who thought Mr Kinnock's performance was like something from a Nuremberg rally. I wasn't offended by the supreme confidence of the Labour party, but I did think that they had gone right over the top when they claimed to be the government in waiting: although, in my opinion, much of the rest of the criticism of the Sheffield rally was simply sour grapes.

DAY 23 THURSDAY 2 APRIL

After the excitement and emotion of the Sheffield rally, Labour intended to draw the competing themes of the election together, ready for the last seven days' campaigning before polling day. In a prepared statement, opening his morning news conference, Neil Kinnock urged people to use their precious civil right to vote. 'It is essential for the vitality of our democracy.' Mr Kinnock's appeal to all voters to participate in the election, whether or not they had made up their minds, was his way of recognising that the last Thursday before polling day had been declared 'democracy day' by the pressure group Charter 88, which was campaigning for constitutional and electoral reform.

Although Mr Kinnock is known to support many of the group's aims, he is always extremely cautious about making a public declaration of support because his party is divided on Charter 88's key objective of seeking to create 'a fair electoral system of proportional representation.' Under Mr Kinnock's guidance the party was steering a difficult course. They were trying to reconcile the competing arguments for and against abandoning the United Kingdom's long tradition of electing, as members of parliament, the candidate who gets the most votes in each constituency; the system known as first past the post.

However, because of the growing demand for change, Labour were preparing to make significant constitutional amendments, should they be elected. The manifesto promised to replace the House of Lords with a new elected second chamber; to introduce fixed term parliaments at Westminster; and to create a Scottish parliament to be elected by the 'additional member system.' There was also an undertaking to enhance the status of Labour's working party under Professor Raymond Plant, who was already examining future electoral systems for Westminister, including proportional representation.

The whole package was put together with great care because of Labour's internal sensitivities. They did not want to damage their own chances but they wanted, at all costs, to avoid being dragged into speculation about a hung parliament and the likelihood, or not, of doing a deal with Paddy Ashdown. The party was well aware that this was dangerous territory because Paddy Ashdown was making electoral reform a pre-condition of any post-election pact.

Liberal Democrats were adamant about their demand for a fairer electoral system, having felt cheated for years. In the 1987 general election, fighting as the Liberal SDP Alliance, they secured 23% of the vote but ended up with only 22 MPs. The sense of grievance was even greater in the Green Party. In the 1989 European elections the Greens attracted two million votes, a 15% share, but failed to get a single seat in the European parliament.

Knowing the background to Labour's internal dissent, we all expected Mr Kinnock, despite it being 'democracy day,' not to get drawn into speculative answers which would only add fuel to the discussion over a hung parliament. The apparent surge in support for the Liberal Democrats made an inconclusive election result seem all the more likely and the perceived strengthening of Mr Ashdown's bargaining position was a regular news conference question. To our surprise, when asked about his latest position on electoral reform, Mr Kinnock expanded on the manifesto commitment. He said that once in government 'people from other political parties' would be offered the chance to participate in Labour's enquiry, known as the Plant committee.

An offer of this kind was perhaps already implicit in the manifesto pledge to give the Plant committee 'an extended membership.' But Mr Kinnock's unexpected reference to 'other political parties' inevitably encompassed the Liberal Democrats and in an election climate, the immediate interpretation was that the Labour leader was offering an olive branch to Mr Ashdown. From the moment he gave that answer Mr Kinnock was on the defensive: he raised the damaging spectre of a Lib–Lab pact and worse still he steered himself straight into the middle of the argument over proportional representation. I sensed that Mr Kinnock was about to repeat the prevarication that he displayed over nuclear disarmament or at the beginning of the miners' strike when it was impossible to divine what his real views were. And now he reached for the political prop which he'd made his own then: obfuscation.

Like many journalists I've wondered for years why Mr Kinnock frequently gives convoluted answers when faced with difficult questions on sensitive issues. I knew he was capable of cutting through prevarication in an instant and expressing himself with the utmost clarity. On a number of occasions in the past, when Julie Hall has telephoned me to complain about one or other of my broadcasts, I have heard Mr Kinnock shouting in the background, telling her exactly what to say.

At the start of the election campaign, I read an interview with Mr Kinnock by Hugo Young in *The Guardian*. Mr Kinnock explained that his verbosity was a tactic which he deployed on purpose when trying to pull the Labour party back from the brink of oblivion. A degree of obscurity meant he could defend and attack at the same time. 'I was never going to let the party down by making a direct answer when that would have generated internal confusion and slowed down the process of change.' Therefore, agreed Mr Kinnock, he used 'longer sentences with more sub-clauses than might otherwise have been strictly necessary.'

I remembered Hugo Young's interview as I sat at the news conference. I knew Mr Kinnock's answer on electoral reform would almost certainly have been discussed, and perhaps approved, by his close adviser and former press secretary Patricia Hewitt. The Institute for Public Policy Research, of which she was deputy director, supported Charter 88 in calling for proportional representation. However, I could not undestand why Mr Kinnock chose that moment, seven days from polling day, to make a public gesture to what were, after all, only pressure groups. I sensed Mr Kinnock was in danger of gradually sliding down the slippery slope towards verbosity. I wondered how long it would take.

News of the supposed 'olive branch' to the Liberal Democrats led the lunchtime news bulletins. Mr Ashdown interpreted it as a sign that Labour were 'wobbling on the fence.' He called on Mr Kinnock to make a decision and say whether or not he accepted proportional representation: 'Labour simply can't go into this election, on this democracy day, saying maybe. It's got to be yes or no.'

Labour had already arranged a second news conference at which Roy Hattersley was to enlarge on the manifesto commitment to constitutional reform. Supporters of Charter 88, whose 29 000 signatories included a large number of Liberal Democrats, lined up outside, handing out leaflets. They were delighted with Mr Kinnock's promise. However, it fell to Mr Hattersley to try to quell mounting speculation over a possible pact. He insisted Labour's Plant enquiry was long term and not a response to the Liberal Democrats. A change in the electoral system could not be 'cobbled together for the convenience of one political party, nor can it be the product of backstairs haggling.'

Mr Ashdown could not hide his delight that Labour, like the Conservatives the previous day, were now marching slap bang into the range of Liberal Democrat gunfire. By the early evening news bulletins, Mr Kinnock was firmly in Mr Ashdown's sights: he asked Labour to come off the fence, otherwise the invitation to other parties would be seen as a fudge: 'It's designed to hint. It's designed to nudge. I don't believe the British people will take a fudge on this great issue.'

The first interviewer to get the chance to follow Mr Ashdown's question through was Sir Robin Day on *This Week*. He lured Mr Kinnock, little by little, like a poacher tickling a trout. Finally, with the crunch question, the Labour leader revealed how firmly he had impaled himself on the hook of proportional representation. Mr Kinnock refused to reveal his own views. 'If I had said what my conclusions were on electoral systems it would translate a constructive activity into a test of loyalty to me as leader. That would be seen by the news media as indicating a party of splits and divisions. I want to hear other people's views.'

The shadow cabinet was bitterly divided over proportional representation so Mr Kinnock could not say yes or no. Either answer might detonate a last minute row, wrecking party unity. But why did

Mr Kinnock choose to sit on the fence on which he was now starting to twist and turn? I knew every interviewer would want to follow Sir Robin by trying to tease out a response. However, the sight of Mr Kinnock floundering would inevitably be grist to the Tory mill: further proof, in their eyes, that the Labour leader was a man without principles who could not be trusted, ready to change his mind for the sake of a quick political fix.

My view that Labour could destabilise their campaign because of the inability to answer the proportional representation question was not accepted immediately by David Hill. He said that a large number of Labour candidates would be taking part in Charter 88 debates during 'democracy day.' 'We want them to have something positive to say. With the electoral reform issue coming up in the news this is a sensible piece of news management. It is part of democracy day.'

Mr Hill rejected suggestions that Mr Kinnock was trying to line up a deal with the Liberal Democrats in the event of a hung parliament. 'We are not bidding for a deal with Paddy Ashdown. But, yes, we are saying to Liberal Democrats whose votes might be soft, and to Conservatives as well, that Labour have an open mind on electoral reform and we favour a consensual approach on the constitution.'

I was puzzled by Mr Hill's answers. I was sure Labour's strategy was flawed. They were generating a rash of hypothetical questions on pacts and proportional representation which would distract their attention from other issues, like the strident build up in the Conservatives' assault on their tax plans.

Labour's tactic of trying to woo Liberal Democrats, while keeping their options open on electoral reform, provided unexpected, but welcome, ammunition for the Conservatives. Mr Major made a combined attack on the other two parties, warning of the dangers of a Lib–Lab coalition, while promising that only the Conservatives could deliver strong government and safeguard the constitution. He described Mr Ashdown as the door keeper to a Labour Britain. 'Don't let Mr Ashdown open that door for Mr Kinnock.'

Mr Major emphatically rejected proportional representation. 'All over Europe where there are proportional representation governments, you tend to have weaker governments than you do when you have a government with a clear majority. There are a number of European governments who would like to get rid of proportional representation because they cannot take firm decisions: they are not strong governments.'

Cabinet ministers were convinced that Mr Kinnock had tripped up. Kenneth Baker told me that the Labour leader had blundered. 'Kinnock is ahead in the polls. So he doesn't need to make a move like this. But it's exactly what we need: proof that all the Lib–Lab nonsense could come back.' Mr Baker was more confident about the Tory campaign than at our last meeting. 'I think we are doing better. We are more confident today and we have got some bounce back into the campaign – but we need a lot more.'

Despite behind the scenes efforts to repair relations, the *Daily Mail's* editor Sir David English was not present when Mr Major visited the Ideal Home Exhibition which the paper sponsors. Sir David's absence renewed speculation that he was still smarting over the way the *Daily Express* got the tip off in the saga of Jennifer's ear. In a statement afterwards the paper said Mr Major's visit was arranged at short notice by the exhibition organisers. Sir David was not informed of the prime minister's presence and therefore had not planned to attend.

Conversations with *Daily Mail* journalists continued to reveal a lack of enthusiasm for Mr Major's campaign. 'Back at the office they think Major is finished. We are just going through the motions at the moment. There's nothing we can do to save him.' However I heard later that Sir David and the prime minister were to meet before the weekend. By calling in friendly political editors Mr Major was acknowledging that he needed more support from the Tory newspapers. From what I could gather, he was now giving this problem the highest priority.

A device used by Labour to pull their election policies together, was to present them in the form of a legislative programme for their first 100 days in office. Jack Cunningham opened the morning news conference with a flourish. He declared that the Labour government's Queen's speech would be on 6 May. Within a matter of weeks John Smith would introduce his budget and by the summer recess Labour would have secured the second reading of bills to abolish all versions of the poll tax, establish a Scottish parliament and introduce a freedom of information act.

For the news media the dominant issue remained the prospect of a hung parliament. Realising he had made heavy weather of the subject, Mr Kinnock displayed a lighter touch when asked again if Labour were trying to do a deal with Paddy Ashdown. 'It is not an overture, not an intermezzo, not even the opening chords. So the idea that this whole process has been conceived in order somehow to creak open the door to the Liberals has got no substance at all.' Mr Kinnock would not reveal his personal preference on proportional representation. He said he intended keeping his opinions to himself for some time longer.

Labour's defensiveness provided a ready made target for Michael Heseltine. He mocked Labour's guile in attempting to seduce the Liberal Democrats by offering talks on electoral reform. 'Why has this ploy been dreamed up overnight? Because the Labour party know they aren't going to win this campaign on their own.' Chris Patten went for the Labour leader. He claimed Mr Kinnock's refusal to say where he stood on proportional representation showed he would 'do anything and sell anything to try and buy votes.'

Mr Ashdown's tactic was to raise the stakes, to build up the prospect of the Liberal Democrats holding the balance of power. He warned that if either Labour or the Conservatives tried to go it alone in a hung parliament they faced the threat of destruction. 'If, in a hung parliament, they put the interests of their party before those of the country they will deserve to go, and sooner or later they will have to go.'

As the day progressed Mr Kinnock realised the awfulness of his position. He looked tired and his cough sounded bad. Important television and radio interviews lay ahead. They were crucial. Viewers and listeners would get the chance to see and hear the real Mr Kinnock, not the twisted words which they might read in a newspaper. Survey after survey showed the importance of television and radio in the formation of people's political views. Labour wanted the interviews to be used by Mr Kinnock as a showcase for himself and for their policies. Their worst fear was that he might become trapped in the byways of the tortuous, sensitive subject of proportional representation and then he would grasp for his tried and tested prop: verbosity.

James Naughtie on *The World At One* got the first chance to develop Sir Robin Day's line of questioning. Was the offer to work for a consensus on constitutional reform opening the door towards a deal in the event of an inconclusive election result and a hung parliament? As if by reflex Mr Kinnock spoke in the obscure way he adopts, as he said himself, when avoiding a direct answer.

'Well the problem is Jim that you speak of it as a hypothesis. So it is. And there are many times in the electoral calendar when we could have such a hypothetical discussion, but not six days before a general election. Because to even enter into the hypothetical discussion makes it difficult for people to separate that from the realities of the conduct of the campaign, the programme we are setting forward, the constructive ideas we have got and what is basically an academic, in the best sense of the word, discussion. So I won't even enter upon the hypothesis.'

Hypothetical or not, it was Mr Kinnock who, only seven days before polling day, set in motion this heightened interest in hung parliaments and electoral reform. Later that afternoon he pre-recorded a *Newsnight* interview. Jeremy Paxman followed up Roy Hattersley's assertion that even if a future Labour government endorsed proportional representation, the subsequent general election would still have to be fought on a first past the post system. Mr Kinnock agreed this was quite probable because the British people would have to decide on any change in the electoral system. In response to a question about whether there could be a referendum on the issue, within a year or two, Mr Kinnock agreed one might be held:

'Oh I think it is possible to do it – you asked me the question about what Roy said – and I said it was quite conceivable that it would not be just this election but a further election that would be on the first past the post system. What I am not going to do, since my whole activity has been dedicated to getting the facts laid out so we can have a very well informed debate and interest and eventually a decision reached by the British people, not by any assertion or feat of politicians, what I am not going to do in those circumstances is to stipulate deadlines, thresholds and try in any way to determine the conclusion of that debate. You and I will know when the debate has risen to the point where it is unavoidable for political parties to make decisions, to make their recommendations and to put the choices before the people. That is one of the reasons why I have strongly favoured spreading the membership of the Plant committee, so it doesn't just involve politicians from one party or even from political parties but also people from the churches, business, trade unions and so on.'

Mr Kinnock's final interview of the day was for *News at Ten*. ITN's political editor Michael Brunson steered clear of pacts and hung parliaments. Mr Kinnock was relieved to get back to basics, claiming the Conservatives' negative approach showed they were ashamed of their record. Mr Brunson asked an astute question about Mr Kinnock himself. How did the Labour leader respond to the fact that he was strongly disliked by some people? At once Mr Kinnock was brief, engaging and self-effacing: 'Politics is a matter of likes and dislikes. If people really want to address the problems of this country, get jobs and build homes, I am prepared to put up with the fact that there is an absence of universal love, as long as people accept that I am in politics to serve my country.'

Shortly after the ITN interview I was speaking to David Hill on the telephone. I knew he was weary of answering my questions about Labour's sudden lurch towards electoral reform. He immediately asked me if I had seen *News at Ten*. 'Did you see Neil being interviewed by Michael Brunson? That was Neil's best interview of the day. He took every question and ran with it. He got his message across every time. Not a word was wasted.' I smiled to myself, not commenting on the implication of what I was hearing. I knew how Mr Hill and all the other spin doctors, those masseurs of the political message, could so easily take offence. The spin I was putting on Mr Hill's remarks was that Labour were finally realising that they must try to keep Mr Kinnock well away from proportional representation and get him back to the bread and butter issues of the campaign.

Labour's opponents exploited the lack of straight answers. Jim Sillars, deputy leader of the Scottish Nationalists, claimed Mr Kinnock would do anything to become prime minister. 'He'd even boil his granny down for glue to get the key to Number 10 Downing Street. And on proportional representation he'll neither say he's for it, nor will he say he's against it. He's just fishing around for votes, and we regard that as a contemptible position.'

Mr Ashdown was in his element, seizing every opportunity to parade the possibility of partnership government. The cornerstone of a coalition would have to be a commitment in the first Queen's speech to legislate on proportional representation. Liberal Democrats would not shirk their responsibility to work for stable government. By contrast Mr Major renewed his promise to govern firmly. He said Labour were showing that they lacked the authority to run the country. 'What a show of confidence we have had from Labour. Cuddling up to the Liberals for support is like leaning on candyfloss.'

Mr Kinnock's indecisiveness provided the perfect trailer for the

Conservatives' next election broadcast. Archive footage was used to illustrate the occasions when the Labour leader had changed his mind. The punch line was hardly new: the people of Britain could not trust 'a man who will change any principle, abandon any policy, say anything, to get elected.' However, despite the familiarity of the content, the Conservatives' broadcast, prepared by Saatchi and Saatchi, was a departure in one respect.

Journalists were given a preview at Tory Central Office. By now we were all weary of this form of electoral communication. The broadcast opened with a series of short answers, delivered by different people, but cut together to make a rapid and spontaneous introduction. Television and radio frequently use this device when trying to reflect the opinions of people in the street. Such interviews are known by broadcasters as 'vox pops.' Saatchi and Saatchi's 'vox pops' were not of British voters, but of people in France, Germany, Italy and Holland. They were all speaking in English, although in the exaggerated continental accents so favoured by the producers of television commercials. Their comments were up-beat and positive: they were talking about a prosperous country with a good government track record. The point of the sequence was to identify the country they were talking about. At the moment of greatest suspense one journalist shouted out 'Albania.' But by then the answer was pretty obviously Britain, although the broadcast said that Labour was not willing to recognise Britain's achievements.

We were all expecting a particularly vicious personal attack on Mr Kinnock. There were rumours that the Conservatives were keeping something nasty up their sleeves. However, as the references to Mr Kinnock seemed rather predictable, most of my colleagues were on the point of departing. At that moment I was talking to Steve Hilton who, although only in his early twenties, was a campaign coordinator for Central Office, responsible for liaison with Saatchi and Saatchi. I could see Mr Hilton was excited as if expecting to say something. Andrew Lansley, the director of the research department, beckoned to a group of journalists, myself included, and told Mr Hilton he had permission to reveal his secret.

We were told the version of the broadcast we previewed was not complete. When transmitted on television later in the evening it would include a flashing message. This would tell viewers to ring Labour if they recognised the country. A telephone number for Labour's London headquarters would also appear on the screen. Mr Hilton said the broadcast was making a serious point: 'We are telling voters who are fed up with the way Labour is knocking Britain to ring up Labour headquarters if they wish to protest. There is something people can do.'

I was intrigued by the audacity of the broadcast but not surprised it was sanctioned by the party leadership. At the Conservatives' annual conference in October, Mr Patten told delegates to jam the switchboards of broadcasting organisations to protest about biased news bulletins and programmes. In November, the party's monthly newspaper, *Conservative Newsline*, published a list of the relevant telephone numbers.

Once news of the election broadcast became public, Labour protested about possible incitement, seeking legal advice. However, the broadcasting organisations said they were powerless to stop transmission because there was nothing unlawful in publicising Labour's telephone number. Responsibility for the content of election broadcasts rests with the parties. Labour maintained it was a pathetic prank. Some calls were abusive, but other callers made telephone donations to the Labour party totalling £5000.

While we were unravelling the Saatchi and Saatchi broadcast, the prime minister's campaign coach drew into Smith Square. Elinor Goodman, Channel 4's political editor, managed to grab a few words with Mr Major. She enquired whether, as he was travelling around 'vacuum packed' in his campaign bus, he might not be sufficiently aware of what was really going on. Startled by her bluntness, Mr Major insisted that the opinion polls which put Labour in front were wrong. He described the warmth of the crowds he was meeting. Miss Goodman told him they were probably people who 'just wanted to touch someone famous.'

When I emerged from Central Office, with Peter Allen, an ITN political correspondent, Miss Goodman was still recovering from her own audacity. It was clear that her only regret was that the exchange was not recorded on camera. By now it seemed every correspondent had a story to tell. Mr Allen recounted with evident pleasure how he slipped a reference into one report about the prime minister finding soapbox campaigning 'very agreeable.' It had become one of those Major expressions that comedians were mimicking.

However, Adam Boulton, political editor of *Sky News*, felt there was an imbalance in television coverage. Because of a tightly controlled campaign, and the reluctance of minders to let him to get too close to reporters, Mr Kinnock was rarely appearing in risky situations. Therefore Mr Boulton thought greater prominence should be given to those occasions when Mr Kinnock appeared over confident or even cocky. When such incidents did occur he thought they were not getting enough exposure.

Sky News had used one incident extensively to show what Mr Boulton felt was a sneering side to Mr Kinnock. Mr Boulton was talking about the Barbour jacket incident, which other television channels did not have the air time to use on this particular day. Mr Kinnock was asked to comment on Edwina Currie's observation that by driving around in a Daimler he was appearing prime ministerial, while Mr Major, who put on his anorak and stood in the rain on his soapbox, was looking like the leader of the opposition. Mr Kinnock interrupted to say that Mr Major was only wearing 'a second rate Barbour.' Mr Boulton felt that this comment showed Mr Kinnock in a very bad light. 'In one breath Mr Kinnock says he wants opportunity for everyone and in the next he suggests that if you can only afford an imitation Barbour, you are second class, not up to it.' Mr Boulton explained that he decided to use this incident on *Sky News* because he felt it showed a cocky side to Mr Kinnock. 'It was the bullying kind of remark you'd hear in a children's playground.' The assembled journalists had laughed at Mr Kinnock's remarks. He was enjoying himself. 'I am just composing a letter in my head about the quality of Mr Major's jacket. I would hate him to think he was under personal attack as well as being hit by eggs,' said Mr Kinnock.

DAY 25 SATURDAY 4 APRIL

As on previous Saturdays, opinion poll predictions were the main preoccupation. By early evening details were available from six separate polls on voting intentions, all commissioned by Sunday newpapers. In order to ensure at least one favourable result, the Conservatives published the findings of their own survey, conducted by Gallup, which examined business opinion. Ninety per cent of those responding thought the Conservatives had the best long term programme for the economy.

John Major said the message was clear: only his government could make the economy hum again. While the prime minister was speaking, photographers tried to capture him in profile against the Conservatives' final election poster. It pictured a smiling Mr Major in a group shot, with three schoolchildren under the slogan 'The Best Future for Britain.' For the remaining days of the campaign the poster was displayed on every one of the 7000 billboard sites hired by the Conservatives.

Tim Collins, press secretary on the campaign coach, assured me Mr Major was a 'very chirpy chappie' because MPs in the marginal constituencies were telephoning him to say their support was firm. They were finding there was strong reaction on the doorsteps against Labour, and considerable criticism of the triumphalism displayed by Labour at their rally in Sheffield. 'Pensioners are telling us that they felt real fear when Kinnock shouted "We're all right." Labour's spin doctors must have been sawing through their wrists when that happened.'

I sat next to Sir Robin Day, who enjoyed himself attending the news conferences, and who on this occasion was also harsh in his criticism of Labour's tactics. He felt Mr Kinnock was wrong to have made the move he did on electoral reform. Labour should have realised it would appear like an overture to Paddy Ashdown, implying that Labour might do a deal in a hung parliament. 'I am afraid Mr Kinnock was very verbose when I interviewed him. He never ended a sentence. I had six pages of notes of questions which I never had a chance to ask.'

At Labour's media centre, David Hill was sticking to his line that people were not confused by Labour's position. 'We are offering the country a chance to participate in a debate on electoral reform. I accept that there is a risk in doing that. But our message will appeal to Liberal Democrats and uncommitted voters.'

When the opinion poll results came through, Mr Hill said Labour remained well placed. Five of the polls put Labour in front, by between two and six points, and the sixth had them level pegging with the Conservatives. When all the percentages were averaged out in the BBC's poll of polls, Labour had a 40% share, the Conservatives had a 37% share, and the Liberal Democrats had a 19% share of the vote.

Mr Hill acknowledged that Labour needed to push a little harder. 'We know who our target group is. It is the undecideds and the wavering Liberal Democrats. We are telling floating voters that they can feel comfortable under Neil Kinnock. The Tories have lost and we are poised to win.'

Des Wilson's assessment was that voters were saying they would accept a hung parliament. 'We intend to speak directly to the public on the advantages of shared government. We will also try to raise the stakes and force the other parties to address the prospect of coalition government. If Labour and the Conservatives don't respond that should help us even further.'

My final mission on this last Saturday of the campaign was to interview Chris Patten. It was 8 pm by the time I reached Central

Office. Except for two receptionists and three security guards, the foyer was deserted. A television set flickered in the corner. I joined the others who were idly watching the James Bond movie *Live and Let Die*. Mark Webster, an ITN political correspondent, arrived for his interview with Mr Patten. Minutes later we were joined by the party's head of broadcasting, Sean Holden. We chatted away about what the result might be. On the basis of the opinion polls, the Conservatives' prospects were bleak and the outlook for party workers rather dispiriting. If they lost, Mr Holden thought he might try getting back into television.

When Mr Patten emerged he was accompanied by a large entourage, including his special adviser Patrick Rock and press officer Angie Bray. We walked across to the church in the middle of Smith Square. The camera crews set up their equipment. We waited on the steps of St John's – used regularly for television interviews because they overlooked Central Office. On countless occasions Mr Patten stood on the same spot answering question after question. The demand for a constant supply of short, sharp answers for television and radio news bulletins sometimes renders the task of collecting these soundbites into a pretty meaningless occupation. I find the whole exercise can be particularly futile on long running news stories when the answers are likely to be utterly predictable.

As we waited I sensed Miss Bray was on edge. Soon after my last interview, when Mr Patten seemed so depressed, I discovered she was concerned that the chairman could sometimes look moody. I wondered how he might be feeling this evening when none of the six opinion polls put the Tories in front. Mr Patten listened patiently for the inevitable first question, seeking his reaction. He began his answer: 'Oxford won the boat race . . .' At this point Mr Patten collapsed in a fit of uncontrollable giggles and staggered out of microphone range. He turned to his advisers: 'Look you lot, stop laughing. You fed me that line. Let me try and get it right.' Take two. 'Oxford won the boat race and we will win the general election.'

CHAPTER 7

SUNDAY 5 APRIL DAY **26**

The opinion polls caused considerable confusion and uncertainty because they continued to predict wide variations in the size of the Labour lead. Over 50 separate polls had been published and every fluctuation cast new doubt on what was really happening. The Conservatives insisted that the volatility of the polls strengthened their argument that there was still everything to play for. But when the percentages for each party were averaged out, Labour were ahead but not by enough to give Neil Kinnock an outright victory.

Most political correspondents were having as much difficulty as I was establishing what was going on. The ups and downs in the polls unsettled us and made it very hard to assess the situation. And there were hosts of contradictory signals emerging from the campaigns. I was struck by the deepening gloom among most journalists on the Tory newspapers. They kept saying that the Conservatives were in turmoil behind the scenes and in their view the tactics Mr Major was adopting were as disastrous as those adopted for Labour's campaign in the 1983 election. In rare moments, Conservative party workers confirmed as much. One said that he could smell defeat inside Tory Central Office.

On the other hand Labour's repeated prediction that they would win a clear overall majority was not convincing. I kept wondering whether Labour really had their eye on the ball. Constitutional issues are of little interest to most people, least of all the reportedly large

numbers of floating voters, but the party leadership was as mesmerised as we journalists were by the polls. If all the opinion polls were
correct Labour's use of electoral reform to squeeze the undecideds,
in the hope of winning the extra 2% to 3% of the vote needed for an
outright majority, made sense.

However the Conservatives' attack on Labour's tax plans was
having considerable effect. Conversations with colleagues revealed
that we were all calculating how much additional income tax and
national insurance we would pay under a Labour government. The
Conservatives were cunningly playing on our potential anxiety as
well. Their newspaper advertisements made a special point of
including journalists. A list of examples estimated the extra tax to
be paid by six workers under a Labour government. The list showed
the tax that a secretary, a nurse, an electrician, a teacher and an
engineer would pay. The highest paid category was a journalist,
earning £25 000, married with a mortgage, who would have to pay
£2379 a year more tax under a Labour government.

We all knew such calculations were wrong and misleading. They
were based on the Conservatives' spurious budgeting exercise
which estimated that Labour's manifesto commitments would cost
£38 billion. That figure was not mentioned in the advertisements nor
was there any clue how the additional tax was calculated. Nevertheless even bogus calculations have an impact, and if journalists
covering the election were any guide, then voters must also be
making similar calculations and coming to their own conclusions.

I was impressed by John Major's steely persistence: he stuck to his
soapbox. To begin with I thought it was a panic move but I soon
realised that he was successfully building up a reputation for being
something of a street fighter. Whatever we journalists might say,
and we were quite derisive about Mr Major's determination to
continue on his soapbox, soapbox oratory suited him and, more to
the point, helped him look and sound assertive. There was no doubt
in my mind that when he was standing outside in the wind and the
rain, he really meant what he was saying. He displayed dogged

determination, against the odds, and that is a particularly British characteristic which proved very appealing.

He was also finding the material to fit perfectly with his bulldog pose. The continuing hiatus over the likelihood of a hung parliament and the prospect of a degree of independence for Scotland were providing the perfect subjects for soapbox speeches. Mr Major portrayed both possibilities as a threat to the stability of the United Kingdom and its tradition of firm government. On these two issues the stance of the Conservatives was firm and distinct. Mr Major's Sunday afternoon rally at Wembley developed his points about the threat to the United Kingdom and its constitution, and expounded them to reinforce the Conservatives' stand against a United States of Europe. These were the three constitutional battles which threatened the unity of the country, he said.

An innocent bystander perched on the Scottish border looking south to London and then north to Edinburgh could be forgiven for thinking two separate elections were taking place. North of the border much of the running was being made by the Scottish Nationalists whose demand for independence was threatening the three other parties. Labour and the Liberal Democrats were both in favour of going some way towards meeting these demands by establishing an elected Scottish parliament. The Conservatives appeared isolated, opposing any form of devolution.

Mr Major made a virtue of his party's long standing refusal to accept any attempt to divide the union. Tearing Scotland away would be 'the fast route to divorce' between two great nations. A separate tax-raising parliament for Scotland would also set the United Kingdom on the road to bitterness, conflict and separation. 'Can you, dare you, consider the outcome? The walls of this island fortress that are so strong, undermined from within? The United Kingdom untied, the bonds that generations of our enemies have fought and failed to break, loosened by us ourselves? If I could summon up all the authority of the office I now hold through the ages, I would put it in a single warning. The United Kingdom is in danger. Wake up. Wake up now, before it is too late.'

None of us could remember rhetoric like that from Mr Major and there was more to come: his government would not accept moves towards a federal Europe, where power was centralised in Brussels, nor would it countenance proportional representation. 'The other parties may fiddle and flirt with constitutional change for party political gain. This party will not.'

Paddy Ashdown was challenged about his relentless pursuit of proportional representation during lunchtime interviews. The opinion polls showed the Liberal Democrats were maintaining their improved ratings and Paddy Ashdown believed this endorsed their strategy. Later, at a rally, he declared his party was on the brink of an outstanding result. 'We may, in a few days time, have in the House of Commons, a significant parliamentary force both to act in the best interests of the country in the immediate future, and to form a powerful bridgehead for a greater advance towards a Liberal Democrat government this decade.'

Labour were only too anxious to depart from the unpromising territory of constitutional and electoral reform. Mr Kinnock gave his clearest pledge of the campaign on tax when questioned by Jonathan Dimbleby in an interview for *On The Record*. Mr Kinnock said that after Labour's first budget there would be no further rises in the rates of income tax. He insisted the resources would be available to enable Labour to meet their specific first year commitments which had all been carefully costed. After that, provision would depend on performance. 'We won't spend what the nation can't afford. I've also made it very clear that there will be no further changes in the levels of taxation.'

In a second lunchtime interview, for *The World This Weekend*, Mr Kinnock said he was sure he would obtain an overall majority, because local and regional opinion polls being conducted in marginal constituencies were indicating that Labour were doing well. 'That is what has made me confident for weeks past that we will secure a majority government.'

Labour's rally in Sheffield was criticised as being 'triumphalist.' Mr Major insisted that such excesses would not be repeated in the lead up to his address at Wembley. Lyricist Tim Rice led a strong cast of celebrities including the singer Lynsey de Paul, fashion designer David Emmanuel and jockey Bob Champion. The presentation was conversational with none of the razzmatazz which preceded Mr Kinnock's speech. Mr Major echoed the sentiments of Conservatives who considered the staging of Labour's event reminiscent of a German pre-war rally. 'There was something very unBritish about those regimented legions of Labour supporters.'

Labour's final star-studded gathering was intimate and informal. It was held in the atrium at Millbank, two floors down from Labour's media centre. As Sir Richard Attenborough stood by to introduce Mr Kinnock, the comedian Ben Elton dubbed it 'Luvvies for Labour.' Among the performers were the harmonica player Larry Adler, actor Anthony Sher and singer Alison Moyet. Throughout the campaign there were far more celebrity packed events than in previous elections. By parading loyal famous faces, the parties believed they were presenting an attractive image to the public and also collecting votes from fans and supporters of the famous faces who were, as yet, politically uncommitted. The time and effort spent on these arrangements was repaid by extra coverage from broadcasters and, perhaps, by more positive treatment in the newspapers.

Political reports on television sometimes suffer from a lack of new and exciting images. The party spin doctors think their glitzy productions and long line-ups of show biz talent are a remedy which works in their favour. Judging by the great diversity of the cast lists there is plenty of scope for post-election analysis by psephologists. They might discover which group has the greatest pulling power with floating voters: actors and actresses, pop stars, comedians, athletes, fashion designers or other personalities yet to be shamelessly exploited in the quest for votes.

DAY 27   MONDAY 6 APRIL

John Major's emotional appeal to voters not to sleepwalk towards a hung parliament and the break up of the United Kingdom, was a gift for headline writers. 'Wakey! Wakey!' said *The Sun*. But Mr Major was taking a great risk. By acknowledging a potentially inconclusive result to the election, he was handing a dangerous weapon to his political opponents. They could claim that even the prime minister was now envisaging the possibility of a Conservative defeat.

On my way to Central Office that morning I joined a group of newspaper journalists. Among them was Trevor Kavanagh, *The Sun's* political editor. We were walking from the Labour news conference up Great Peter Street towards Smith Square. Mr Kavanagh said ruefully that as Labour had convinced themselves they were the next government, he thought it was time that we all went to hear what the opposition had to say.

We found Mr Major in fighting form. He opened his news conference with a stark warning that Britain would never see strong government again if a coalition between Labour and the Liberal Democrats changed the voting system. He was backed up by Douglas Hurd, the foreign secretary, who said a hung parliament would 'hang the recovery.'

We all knew that the last few days of the campaign were crucial. A catastrophic mistake could instantly tip the result one way or the other. Everyone was on edge. The Conservative news conference was particularly well attended. Many journalists had to stand at the side. The heat of the television lights was uncomfortable. While Mr Major delivered his opening remarks, Mr Hurd slumped forward in his chair, the foreign secretary remained expressionless as though his thoughts were miles away. Chris Patten's face was grey, he seemed to be terribly tired. He shielded his eyes from the glare of the lights with his hand and cast nervously around the room, scanning the faces of the assembled journalists.

Unlike the light and airy setting used by Labour, the news conference room at Central Office is too small for important briefings. The shortage of space means we are cramped and crowded together. The front row of journalists' seats are almost on the platform. Five rows back the television crews with their cameras and lights crowd in. The low ceiling, the lack of natural light and the use of various shades of blue to decorate the room create an overpowering effect. It gets hot and stuffy very quickly. On some days I felt it was like the kind of bunker ministers used in war time. However, in one way, the tense atmosphere worked to the news media's advantage. The discomfort we felt and our close proximity to the party leaders on the platform encouraged confrontational questioning.

Once Mr Patten invited questions, almost every hand went up. We needed no encouragement. This was the moment to go hard on Mr Major and challenge him about a hung parliament. Michael Brunson of ITN got in first, asking the prime minister what he would do if the voters opted for coalition. Mr Major avoided a direct answer. He repeated his point that a weak government would be unable to serve the country. Britain would lack authority when speaking abroad. No chancellor could negotiate in Europe on a single currency while at the same time looking over his shoulder, fearing a minority government might be brought down at any moment.

The next question was from *The Sun*. Mr Kavanagh's long experience in popular journalism means he gets straight to the point: 'It is a cardinal rule in election campaigns that you maintain only one possibility and that is outright victory. That is certainly the case round the corner at Labour. They are very confident this morning. Yet in a speech last night, and in your press conference this morning, you are homing in on the possibility of a hung parliament. Does that not attract at least the possibility that you are admitting – '

At that point Mr Kavanagh was interrupted by the prime

minister. Seeing the significance of this potentially devastating enquiry, coming from a normally friendly quarter like *The Sun*, and sensing that the next word on Mr Kavanagh's lips was probably 'defeat,' Mr Major, grim faced, leant forward and intervened, his voice taking on an urgent pitch: 'I will tell you exactly what it indicates. I have said consistently throughout this campaign that I believe the Conservative party will have a clear working majority for five years. It is not the Conservatives who are flirting with the Liberals over a deal on proportional representation to sustain a government thereafter. I have ruled out deals. I am anxious to maximise the clear majority I believe we will get on Thursday.' It was not the answer but the directness of the question which stopped me in my tracks. I admired Mr Kavanagh's professionalism. His enquiry was brutal but effective. He put Mr Major on the spot. However, I detected a degree of tension in his question. I wondered if this was perhaps a tangible example of the anxiety which I knew some journalists were trying hard to suppress.

Political editors and correspondents on Conservative newspapers were well aware that polling day could be crunch time for them as well as for Mr Major. Like the prime minister they were beneficiaries of the Thatcher years. During her time in Downing Street, Mrs Thatcher guarded and strengthened the links between her party and newspaper proprietors and editors loyal to the Conservative cause. Her ceaseless efforts reinforced the clear dividing line between political journalists working at Westminster. Journalists working for the Tory press have relatively free access to Tory ministers, ministerial advisers or party officials. Broadcasters, or journalists working for news agencies or newspapers which take an independent political line, can face difficulty establishing such contacts.

There is nothing new in newspapers having strong political views and loyalties. The tradition is deeply entrenched in British parliamentary history. Newspaper journalists have every right to expect a degree of preference if their editorial policy matches the political complexion of the party in power. Nevertheless after 13 years of Conservative government, the preferential treatment enjoyed by some journalists has become a way of life. Their access to Conservative ministers and to the heart of the government machine far outstrips that of journalists on the other side of the dividing line.

Because of legislation requiring the political neutrality of the broadcasting organisations, television and radio correspondents are under strict instructions to remain impartial and avoid political links. Consequently the nature of my work can at times be very different from that of newspaper correspondents. I am certainly not subjected to the pressures which they are subject to and to which they often object. They complain on occasion about having no alternative but to write stories which they freely admit are slanted politically.

Persistent forecasts of a Labour victory were responsible for creating the apprehension among Tory journalists who feared their favoured access was about to disappear. Although their worries were rarely expressed publicly, their unease was obviously heightened by Mr Major's willingness to address the possibility of a hung parliament. Unexpectedly I found myself witnessing a sudden flash of anger as a group of Tory journalists remonstrated with a cabinet minister over the inadequacies of the Tory campaign.

We were invited upstairs to a smaller briefing room at Central Office. We were told that David Mellor, chief secretary to the treasury, would be with us shortly to present a new assessment of Labour's economic plans. The wait was longer than expected and we were all becoming impatient. I heard outspoken criticism of Conservative campaign tactics from journalists whose newspapers were closest of all to the Tory party: those newspapers whose political editors formed the 'White Commonwealth.' They felt the campaign was awful, totally negative and lacked a coordinated message. A source of even greater annoyance was that Labour were achieving publicity by promising to spend a few hundred million pounds more on health and education, when government expenditure ran into billions. They could not understand why the Conservatives were not making more of their own spending programmes.

A slight diversion arose when apologies for the delay were given by Michael Gunton, a senior press officer. He was concerned by the rather grim mood of some of the journalists and assured the most outspoken that the Conservatives would win by an unexpectedly comfortable majority. He was ready to put up hard money to back his conviction and offered to take bets on a Tory victory. He found no takers although one journalist said the cost of the bet would be nothing compared with what he would lose in tax under Labour.

Finally Mr Mellor arrived and presented new calculations by the Conservatives' research department. These claimed to show that a Labour government would immediately add a £10 billion surcharge to the costs of British industry. One basis for the estimate was a prediction of a 2.5% interest rate rise the moment Labour were elected. As we sat round the table I could see most of the journalists were looking at Mr Mellor in disbelief. Hardly anyone bothered to challenge him. The calculations seemed too flimsy to be true.

At the end of the briefing I was about to interview Mr Mellor when some journalists began to tell the chief secretary, in pretty blunt language, what they thought about the inadequacies of the Conservative campaign. One of the strongest criticisms was over the failure of the government to promote their own high spending on public services. One journalist summed up their complaint: 'Why are you letting Labour gain credibility? All they are doing is recycling their old pledges. But they are giving the impression they will do something and that you are not doing anything.' Mr Mellor was taken aback at suddenly finding himself the butt of their fury. 'You lot don't seem to understand. It is not easy for us to march to the high ground. I have the greatest sympathy for those people trying to put our campaign together. Everyone knows Labour's promises are only paper thin.'

The journalists felt passionately about what they were saying. However, they did not seem to be speaking from any obvious political conviction. My impression was they were motivated by a recognition that they too would have a lot to lose if the Tories were defeated. A newly elected Labour government would inevitably shut the door on the privileged access which many of the Tory journalists enjoyed. Contacts nurtured with great care would no longer be useful. These journalists would have to find new sources of information in what, for them, would be politically hostile terrain. After 13 years on the inside, they clearly had no wish to be on the outside under Labour.

Eventually the endless speculation over a hung parliament became tiresome even to the Liberal Democrats. Despite their efforts to raise the stakes and force Labour and the Conservatives to face up to the prospect of coalition, they were getting nowhere. Mr Kinnock tried to put Mr Ashdown in his place, telling him to stop engaging in the 'imagined card games' which he thought the Liberal Democrats would be playing after polling day.

Mr Ashdown faced criticism on *Election Call* for implying that his party would put electoral reform above the interests of the nation. He denied that the Liberal Democrats would hold the country to ransom if there was a financial crisis or the prospect of war. In such circumstances his party might support a minority government. 'Sensible people don't close every option. Obviously everybody has to do what they think is right under the circumstances for the country's good.'

Des Wilson, who had seemed so pleased with the direction of the campaign, was irritated by *The Times'* lead story which suggested the Liberal Democrats would demand four seats in the cabinet as the price for supporting a coalition government. Speculation of this kind undermined the attempts of the party leadership to present themselves as principled politicians. Their emphasis on the prospect of a hung parliament had backfired and they found themselves stuck in a cul-de-sac, distracting attention from their other policies. The Liberal Democrats tried to refocus the spotlight on their plan to increase income tax by a penny to pay for improvements in education.

The softening in Mr Ashdown's previously uncompromising attitude came after the Conservatives' news conference. Douglas Hurd's political adviser, Maurice Fraser, told me that despite the reservations of some journalists, the Tories had no alternative but to face the prospect of a hung parliament head on. 'We can't avoid the subject. We have always held strong views on the constitution and it is far better to hit back hard.'

On the campaign coach Simon Brooke, the chief broadcasting officer, wished the party had chosen an economic issue, or perhaps consumer affairs, to tie in with Mr Major's planned visit to a shopping centre near Southampton. As Mr Major walked round the complex, an egg thrown at close range by a demonstrator hit him in the face. The force of the blow caused him to stumble and his face started bleeding from a cut on his cheekbone.

Mr Major was becoming quite an expert at dodging eggs and other assorted missiles and his experiences provided an immediate source of inspiration for his opening chat with David Dimbleby preceding an interview for *Panorama*. He described the latest incident as 'quite nasty.' Until it happened he would never have believed that someone weighing nearly 13 stone could have been knocked over by the force of an egg thrown at close range.

These warm-up conversations were becoming one of the high spots of the campaign. Mr Kinnock discovered only just in time that there was an avid, but invisible, audience for his *Newsnight* interview the previous Friday. Journalists with news deadlines were invited to the pre-recording as usual. They sat in an adjoining room watching on a monitor. After the initial pleasantries Mr Kinnock launched into a story about Peter Hitchens, the *Daily Express* reporter at the centre of the Jennifer's ear saga. Jeremy Paxman instantly stopped Mr Kinnock from going any further, to the disappointment of the eavesdropping journalists who were by now coming to the conclusion that warm-up small talk might soon start providing better story lines than the interviews themselves.

Mr Kinnock faced a tough inquisition later on *World in Action*.

Five hundred voters from two Conservative marginal constituencies: Bolton North East and Bolton West, were invited to put questions to the three party leaders. Mr Major was hissed for refusing to apologise for what one questioner said was the 'misery' of the poll tax. Mr Ashdown insisted that partnership government could get Britain out of recession, but Mr Kinnock ended up being ridiculed for his refusal to give a straight answer on the question of proportional representation.

Right at the start Mr Kinnock apologised for his voice, saying he was still troubled by a terrible cold. But the audience had no sympathy for him when first time voter Alec Dunn, aged 20, persisted in demanding a 'yes' or 'no' answer. Mr Kinnock explained the procedure which Labour were going through and the importance of waiting for the Plant committee's analysis. But the audience joined in to support Mr Dunn shouting: 'Answer in English, not Chinese. Yes or No, a simple answer.' Sue Lawley, the presenter, interrupted to say there were only 15 seconds left, but the programme ended without Mr Kinnock divulging his own preference.

Later, Mr Kinnock expressed satisfaction over the results of the largest opinion poll of the campaign in which 10000 people were questioned for the Press Association. It put Labour ahead by 2.5%. The overall swing to Labour from the Conservatives was 7%, but it was higher in areas like the West and East Midlands where there are important marginal constituencies. Two other opinion polls also put Labour in front. When averaged by the BBC's poll of polls, Labour had a lead of 3%.

On *Channel 4 News* Mr Kinnock insisted there was no complacency in the Labour campaign: 'We are not ... to use the fashionable word ... cocky about it. We will keep on working for and earning our support.' At Labour's media centre, David Hill was convinced their strategy to attract Liberal Democrat voters in the marginal constituencies was paying off. 'There are up to 100 swing seats where we are very confident. Voters know the only way to turn over the sitting Tory MP is to vote Labour. People are thinking tactically in the marginals and realising the power they have. They are saying yes to change. All we need is another 1.5% to win.'

Neil Kinnock's refusal to divulge his personal preference for or against proportional representation returned to haunt the Labour campaign for the fifth day running. The demand of the Bolton voters for an answer 'in English not Chinese' knocked into a cocked hat Saatchi and Saatchi's efforts to make fun of Mr Kinnock's obfuscation. Nevertheless Tory Central Office were determined to try again. In a skit which bore all the hallmarks of *That's Life*, a starring role was found for the party's music hall performer. Chris Patten opened. He said he had been unfair about Mr Kinnock's failure to answer important constitutional questions and wanted the Labour leader's subsequent clarification on *World in Action* to have as wide an audience as possible. Mr Patten called for the assistance of the 'most famous living Welshman.' The Swansea-born Michael Heseltine played Neil Kinnock and Chris Patten played the supporting roles:

Alec Dunn (Patten): Are you in favour of proportional representation? I want to know where you personally stand on the subject.
Neil Kinnock (Heseltine): Well I would be delighted to be able to tell you.
Sue Lawley (Patten): Now.
Kinnock: At this juncture well I would be delighted to, but what, er what do you mean?
Dunn: Either you agree with it or you don't.
Kinnock: Yes sure. Well, quite. No. It is not quite as simple as that, not sitting where I am sitting.
Lawley: You have about 30 seconds to tell them, Mr Kinnock, why you won't say where you stand on this as the other leaders do.

Kinnock: Many times in public ... Exactly, absolutely what my approach has been. It is that two years, two and a quarter years ago, I established a procedure in the Labour party because it is important that we get the analysis and the recommendation on proportional representation.

Lawley: You have 15 seconds Mr Kinnock. They want to know where you stand on PR.

Kinnock: That is what we will do and I find it extraordinary that the current government believes our system incapable of improvement. I refuse to take that view.

Throughout their double act Mr Patten added footnotes like 'uproar in audience.' When a helpful reporter asked why they were both so demob happy the Tories' own Archie Rice replied: 'I tell you we are on our way boyo. We are going to win this election. That is what we are going to do.' Party workers who crowded in to watch the fun applauded heartily. Shaun Woodward's face was one big smile, but he insisted that the sketch was the result of 'collective inspiration.'

Labour's cabaret act was shorter but also had an end of term atmosphere. Health was the subject for their news conference. Mr Kinnock said voters must choose between the break up and privatisation of the NHS under the Conservatives, or its build up and modernisation under Labour. Robin Cook issued a challenge to William Waldegrave. He was concerned that his opposite number had disappeared from the campaign trail after his news conference fiasco during the saga of Jennifer's ear: 'I'm worried about William. I've not seen him out in public for almost a fortnight. I have a challenge for Chris Patten. Will he let William Waldegrave out to debate with me? Just in case the answer is no, I want to add one more commitment to our checklist for our first 100 days in office. On Friday 10 April, we will send out a search party to find and rescue William Waldegrave.' When journalists demanded to know the financial standing of this pledge Mr Cook said: `Yes, resources permitting.'

The three party leaders were all preparing their final appeals to the electorate. Cilla Black topped the celebrity list at the Conservatives' rally. She said Mr Major deserved a 'lorra, lorra' votes because she did not want to go back to 'all those strikes and all those pickets.' Mr Major claimed the election of a Labour government would be a 'massacre of the innocents by the ignorant' because it would result in the 'biggest transfer of wealth away from personal ownership' that Britain had ever seen.

The actor Richard Wilson was Labour's host. Mr Kinnock said voting Conservative would be like calling back a plumber who had failed three times to fix a leak and who had left the customer in the kitchen up to the waist in water.

Paddy Ashdown did not refer to the prospect of a hung parliament, but urged voters not to be put off by Tory scare tactics. He claimed that the Conservatives were undermining the constitution by denying fair representation to minority parties and this was eating 'away at the very vitality of our democracy.' The day ended with further fluctuation in the opinion polls.

The most significant shift was in a Harris survey for ITN. This put Labour on 40%, down a point on the previous week, while the Conservatives were on 38%, up by three points. The Labour lead was cut back by one point.

Labour's failure to develop a consistent national lead, followed by this latest signal which suggested that their support could be ebbing away, mystified party tacticians. Behind the confident facade of the leadership the same doubts that nagged at us lurked. After a radio interview, Roy Hattersley asked my opinion. He thought Labour would win. Like Mr Kinnock, he based his conviction on polling evidence from marginal constituencies, some of which were reporting big Labour swings. But Mr Hattersley was in need of reassurance: 'I am Roy, your friendly bookmaker. Where would you place your bet?'

I was as confused as everyone else. The Conservatives said the latest polls verified their belief that Labour's lead was always unreliable and that the Tory vote was firming up. There was no way of knowing whether opinion polls from the most marginal seats were a reliable guide. Labour, like the other parties, invested much of their campaign effort in these seats but some of the swing seats were getting the kind of news coverage normally reserved for by election campaigns. Heightened local interest was certainly having an impact on constituency polling. If a constituency is in the political limelight, its electorate, when polled, will often say things that they would not say under more normal circumstances. Therefore the significance of what those polled in these constituencies said, was hard to gauge. Mr Hattersley said that he could not understand why Labour's lead was so much higher in some marginals than in others. 'I can't explain it. Why are the marginals behaving so differently?'

Mr Hattersley asked me: 'Have you any idea what the Tory tabloids are up to?' He was distressed by the virulence of their reporting, but puzzled by the fact that in the early stages of the campaign the popular press were preoccupied by other news stories, rarely leading with the election, and certainly not printing as many anti-Labour horror stories as Labour expected. He wondered what was in store for the last two days.

Several of the mass circulation papers were known to be working on lively coverage for the closing stages. The *Daily Mail's* front page was a forerunner. In big capital letters was a one word headline: 'Warning.' Beneath it a large black box contained the following message: 'A Labour government will lead to higher mortgage payments. There is no doubt about it. Interest rates will rise within days of Kinnock entering Number 10.'

DAY **29** WEDNESDAY 8 APRIL

The party machines were pushing local campaigning to fever pitch in the constituencies, ready for polling day. At Westminster the response among politicians and journalists alike was a gradual realisation that there was little more we could do. Further speculation was pointless. The outcome was clearly going to depend on unknown and unpredictable factors, like the size of the turnout or a last minute swing.

We were all exhausted by the non-stop electioneering which, for us, had effectively begun when Mrs Thatcher resigned in November 1990. Since then, we were on the alert in case of a snap election. Finally the end was in sight. The party leaders would soon begin the agonising wait on polling day itself. They were ready to unwind, just a little, and the eve of polling day turned out to be a decidedly friendly day.

Retrospection was the order of business at the morning news conferences. Paddy Ashdown claimed that the Liberal Democrats, by being positive, forced Labour and the Conservatives to retreat from a negative agenda and a purely American style of campaigning. 'We may have helped to turn Britain away from a style of politics which is interminably boring and devastatingly negative.' Neil Kinnock paid tribute to a 'certain vitality' in Mr Ashdown's campaign but considered the change in tactics forced upon the Conservatives revealed the same 'rootlessness' that they demonstrated in government. John Major was surprisingly frank. He accepted that the Conservatives were unlikely to return to Westminister with anything like the 90 seat majority they had in the last parliament. Although confident of a 'clear majority' he conceded that their support would be reduced because people had been hurt by the 'difficulties and bruises' of the recession.

In closing his last news conference, Chris Patten appealed for a reasoned end to the proceedings. Michael White of *The Guardian* promptly asked whether Mr Major, or any cabinet minister on the platform, would take a bet on there not being a 2.5% rise in interest rates if there was a Labour government on Friday. He was ready to wager £100 or £1000 in the case of Mr Heseltine. There were no takers. Mr Patten simply said that £1000 was a great deal less than

The Guardian's political editor would lose in tax under a Labour government.

Earlier, on *Election Call*, Mr Major was forced into a corner about what the Conservatives would do if there was a hung parliament and Labour proposed a Queen's speech. Although he said later that he was drawn into speculation against his better judgment, on *Election Call* Mr Major agreed to study Labour's parliamentary programme and to do what was in the best interests of the country. Immediately afterwards Mr Major was asked to sign an autograph book for the 'Children in Need' appeal. He was teased by the presenter Jonathan Dimbleby about where he would sign his name. 'To the far right of the page?' 'No I think the middle right,' replied Mr Major. The prime minister revealed that he and the Labour leader shared a private joke about where Paddy Ashdown wrote his signature on appeals like these. They always checked to see to which of their names Paddy Ashdown signed his name the closest.

Hearing this pleasant aside reinforced my impression that Mr Major was uncomfortable when publicly accusing Mr Kinnock and the shadow cabinet of being unfit to hold office. When challenged about this by David Frost on TV-am, Mr Major said he was not questioning Mr Kinnock's patriotism but his judgment on the key issues of Europe and defence. On both, Mr Kinnock had changed his mind. Mr Frost pursued his question by quoting from *The Economist* which suggested that Mr Major's 'innate decency' stopped him driving home the point any further. Was this true? Mr Major replied: 'I have nothing more to add. That summarises it accurately.'

However, Mr Major's vision of the horrors of a Labour government as 'A Nightmare on Kinnock Street' found a sequel in the eve of poll issue of *The Sun*. Alongside the front page banner headline 'A Question of Trust' were close up pictures of the eyes of the two leaders: Mr Major's eyes were smiling, they looked normal, whereas Mr Kinnock's eyes looked agitated and alarmed. Captions underneath said readers could have 'no confidence' in Mr Kinnock whereas Mr Major was 'solid and dependable with a cool head.' Eight full pages inside, each under the logo 'Nightmare on Kinnock Street,' gave *The Sun's* account of what life would be like under Labour.

Mr Kinnock faced further abuse on arrival at Blackpool airport. A small plane circled overhead trailing the message: 'Get stuffed boyo.'

Mr Ashdown, determined to live up to his reputation as the most media friendly of the three, tried his hand at a doorstep interview right in the middle of ITN's lunchtime news. Libby Weiner was delivering her report live from the steps of Yeovil Liberal Club when Mr Ashdown walked out, right on cue, and put his arm round her shoulder, saying: 'Now I'm doorstepping you!' Miss Weiner turned the tables, immediately trying to interview Mr Ashdown. Mr Ashdown paid the final compliment: 'Libby, you're never at a loss for words. We knew we wouldn't faze you. It was just a joke.'

On my way to Central Office I kept mulling over a remark of Mr Major's, after *Election Call*, about there being 'a high cock-up factor' among Tory supporters when they were polled. He felt that many traditional Conservative supporters had such a low regard for the pollsters that they might not be giving straight answers or even bothering to reply at all. Nevertheless he thought the trend of the last few days was in their favour and they would get a majority.

The good humour from the three leaders helped dull the suspense. We all knew we could be at another turning point in British politics, but there was nothing for it but to wait. I kept busy testing out the party spin doctors: what gloss were they putting on the conflict in the opinions polls?

Mr Major's campaign press officer, Tim Collins, was convinced that the prediction of the week before, that Labour were seven points ahead, had worked in favour of the Conservatives. 'The size of that lead shocked people and our support started picking up last weekend.' The campaign also dispelled the notion that Mr Major would find an election too strenuous. 'He spent more time talking to ordinary people and meeting journalists than Kinnock did, and he remains a popular figure.' Mr Collins backed up his point by quoting the latest Harris poll showing Mr Major had a two-to-one lead over

Mr Kinnock when people were asked who would make the best prime minister.

The final four opinion polls sent a tremor of excitement through Central Office. Gallup put the Conservatives half a point ahead; ICM put the two main parties neck and neck; MORI put Labour in front by one point; and NOP put Labour three points ahead. But the gap was closing. In the BBC's poll of polls Labour's lead was cut by a further point to 39%; the Conservatives were on 38%; and the Liberal Democrats on 19%.

David Hill's voice was worried when I spoke to him on the telephone but he insisted the polls were not unlike Tuesday's. 'I have just heard from *The Times* that the MORI poll shows the swing in the marginals is still 9% to Labour. I stand four square by what I said last night. Yes, the uniform national swing is pointing to a hung parliament, but the swing in the marginals is still one point more than the 8% we need for an overall Labour majority.'

Half an hour later Mr Hill rang back to say that he had some stunning news: the election day edition of the *Financial Times* was going to back Labour. He gave me the quote: 'The dangers of perpetuating in power a weakened and uncertain Conservative party, set alongside the progress Labour has made in modernising itself, justify, by a fine margin, the risks of a change.' I could sense the pride in Mr Hill's voice: recognition at last of all that had been done under Neil Kinnock's leadership to prepare Labour for the election and for government.

But again I felt an underlying tension in his voice. All the evening news reports were saying that the gap was narrowing: that Labour's lead was down. It seemed heartless to tell Mr Hill his call was too late. There was little use that I as a broadcaster could make of the quote. It was already getting on for 11 pm. The news report I was preparing was for election day morning and it had to be strictly factual: party politics were out and there was nothing more any of the spin doctors could do either. We were on the eve of a cliffhanger.

THURSDAY 9 APRIL – POLLING DAY

Political leaders the world over go through the same ritual on election day as they cast their votes: smiles and handshakes for the photographers and then one last, snappy soundbite for television and radio. A misty dawn promised and delivered a mild spring day. Paddy Ashdown was the first to vote. With his wife Jane and dog Luke they set off on a tour of local polling stations. After that he waited 'with a beating heart' for the result. Neil Kinnock felt fit after his cold. He was ready, as footballers say, to play 'another 90 minutes'. The lapels of Glenys Kinnock's jacket were the colours of Labour's rosette. John and Norma Major posed together for their last photo-call of the campaign. 'Feeling lucky, feeling winning too,' was the prime minister's contribution to the soundbite collection.

The 1992 election was a record breaker: it attracted more candidates and more political parties than any previous general election. Throughout the country there were 2925 candidates. In addition to the hundreds being fielded by the established parties, there were scores of individual candidates standing on their own under a multiplicity of slogans and titles.

My task on election evening was to visit marginal constituencies in London. Like so much of the country, the capital contained a clutch of seats where the Conservatives would have to be beaten if Labour were to form the next government. My tour confirmed what I suspected might be the case throughout the country. In safe Labour and Tory seats there was not much evidence of campaigning but in those constituencies thought most likely to change hands there was a frenzy of activity.

I drove from north to south, through the Conservative-held territory of the outer London boroughs. There was hardly a political poster to be seen: sometimes the odd splash of blue but not much else. Finchley was the first constituency I drove through which still seemed to be in the throes of a lively contest: plenty of posters and a definite buzz in the air.

But the real excitement was closer to inner London. At Labour headquarters in Hornsey and Wood Green no one could spare the time to speak. Inside the office I could see members of the campaign team holding telephones. They were busily ringing round, working through their lists of promised votes, reminding people to vote. A few miles further on I detected an air of quiet confidence at Glenda Jackson's campaign office for Hampstead and Highgate. Fresh volunteers were still arriving although the polling stations would close in little over an hour.

South of the river, in Dulwich, there was no need to ask questions at Labour headquarters. As soon as they realised I was a journalist, party workers chanted: 'It's definitely bye, bye Bowden.' They were confident that Labour would retake the seat from the Conservatives, overturning Gerald Bowden's tiny majority of 180. Further west in Battersea, Labour's campaign team were in high spirits but nowhere near so confident. A poll tax rate of zero was presenting Labour with an uphill struggle in the parliamentary constituencies of the London Borough of Wandsworth.

Despite driving round some of London's swing seats, talking to party workers, I found I was still as uncertain as before about the likely outcome. Election nights are often like this. After being so close to a story for so long, trying to understand and absorb an enormous amount of information, a dispassionate assessment proves elusive. My sense of expectation was tremendous but I could not make a snap judgment. The closest parallel was with the way I felt on polling day in 1970, when Edward Heath won what became known as the 'shopping basket' election.

My task in that campaign, as a parliamentary correspondent for *The Times*, was to report the speeches of Sir Alec Douglas-Home, then shadow foreign secretary, as he toured the country. Each evening, after Central Office supplied him with details of the latest price increases for groceries and other household goods, Sir Alec would manfully include the shopping basket list in his speech, trying desperately not to get the pounds and ounces muddled up with the pounds, shillings and pence. I could tell he did not have much faith in the strategy. It certainly did not make much of an impression on me. When the campaign ended I felt Sir Alec had very little expectation of a Conservative victory. But the Tories' aim, of appealing to housewives, paid off and Edward Heath defeated Harold Wilson.

In this election the Conservatives were deploying the same kind of tactic: a constant drip feed of warnings about tax increases under Labour. I kept thinking that this strategy was almost certainly having the same effect as in 1970, but would it be enough to destroy Labour's opinion poll lead? When my broadcast was completed, I stopped off for a few minutes outside Labour's national headquarters, down the road from the Elephant and Castle. But soon I was on my way, heading back to Westminster and Smith Square. The only place for me that night was Tory Central Office, because so much was at stake for the Tory party. I frequently felt riveted to the spot during the campaign, so gripping were the events unfolding around me.

Inside the news conference room there was already a hive of activity. I arrived just before 11 pm. Dozens of journalists and technicians were milling about. All the chairs had been removed and staff from each of the television and radio stations were staking out their own patch of territory, ready to broadcast live reports. Television sets along one side of the room were tuned to the competing election night programmes.

Just after I arrived the first result came through: at 11.05 pm Chris Mullin was returned as Labour MP in Sunderland South but with a swing of only 2.5% to Labour, nothing like the opinion poll predictions. Next to declare was Torbay where Rupert Allason's majority was well over 5000 despite a 3.2% swing to the Liberal Democrats.

Shaun Woodward and his colleagues from the communications department were nervously patrolling the room, exchanging only the odd word or two with journalists. I could tell they were desperate to hear more results. Suddenly someone shouted: 'Basildon is being declared.' This was the first of the marginals where Labour had to beat the Conservatives. There was an immediate hush. Everyone strained to look at the nearest television set.

Once the result was announced and it was clear David Amess was safely back, there were looks first of disbelief and then sheer joy on the faces of the Tory press officers and the Central Office staff. I heard someone shout out: 'It's tremendous.' I found myself being berated by a party worker who had joined the throng: 'You all thought Essex man had deserted us, didn't you? Well, he hasn't.' The swing against the Conservatives was only 1.3%, nowhere near what Labour needed. We all watched as Mr Amess delivered his victory speech: 'I must be doing something right and the Conservative government must be doing something right as well.' For a moment the sound of the Tory cheers in Basildon seemed to reverberate round the room in central London.

A procession of senior Tories were lining up on television to give their comments. Kenneth Baker thought Labour peaked too quickly: 'They held their coronation in Sheffield and we fought back.' But soon there were some Labour gains. Pendle changed hands on a 4.5% swing. Next to be interviewed was Jack Cunningham. He said the results were showing the Conservatives had lost the authority to stay in office. Twenty minutes later came the Cheltenham declaration: the Liberal Democrats took the seat from the Conservatives. Labour gained Hyndburn and Nuneaton. Robin Cook claimed it would be offensive for a government to try to stay in office after having been hit by such a sharp swing. But many of the seats which Labour wanted were staying blue. After holding Putney with an increased majority, David Mellor delivered his victory speech: 'Putney has taken an irrevocable decision tonight and will never go back to the Labour party.'

At this point Mr Woodward agreed to give us a briefing. He looked pleased and relaxed. 'Obviously we are still taking it constituency by constituency, but Labour just aren't getting the seats they need. It's looking very good indeed.' He thought the results in the south east underlined the strength of the Tory attack on Labour's tax plans. 'We were so right to go hard on a hung parliament because it kept Labour bogged down on proportional representation. That was the worst thing they did. Once they got hooked on all that nonsense about electoral reform they got trapped in Paddy's agenda and just couldn't get back to the issues. They simply lost sight of the ball and never recovered.'

As Mr Woodward was speaking we could see Mr Kinnock arriving for his constituency declaration. A few minutes later ITN predicted an overall Conservative majority of seven seats, amending their previous forecasts of a hung parliament. Two reporters hurried back into the building from their posts outside in Smith Square. They said that Tory party workers were showing their first signs of confidence; they were hanging up blue and white balloons outside Central Office. It was 1.31 am.

Although television predictions of the likely size of the Conservatives' majority were increasing all the time, Mr Woodward and his staff looked around anxiously on being told that Chris Patten's declaration was imminent. As the election programmes switched to Bath no one spoke. We all crowded round the television sets.

The moment we saw close ups of Mr Patten's face we guessed that he knew his result. He looked completely shattered. His gaze was fixed firmly ahead. He pursed his lips as the figures were announced. The Liberal Democrats took the seat with a majority of 3768. Mr Patten thanked local people for their kindness and courtesy in the

13 years he had been their MP. He promised that the 'Conservative flag will fly over Bath once again.' Sitting beside me, looking distraught, was Vanessa Ford, the press officer assigned to Mrs Major. Mr Woodward paid an immediate tribute on behalf of Central Office: 'At a moment when everything seems to be going so well for the party, we are extremely saddened to see Chris defeated. He was the architect of our campaign. He inspired us all.'

There were repeated tributes to Mr Patten on the election programmes and also praise for the Conservatives' campaign. Michael Heseltine thought their tactics had turned out to be brilliant. To win an election in the depths of the recession when bad economic news was pouring down 'like bricks from heaven' was an incredible performance.

Norman Lamont thought their attack on Labour's tax plans had been getting through to voters all the time but was simply not showing up in the polls. This was supported by Mr Patten's adviser Patrick Rock. 'Obviously if someone is asked by a pollster if they favour spending on the NHS or tax cuts they are not going to appear a selfish swine, so they say they support the NHS. But don't forget that we knew from our tax campaign in January that if we kept stating and restating the tax figures, they would eventually be driven home and have the desired effect.' Mr Rock told me that the 'Kinnock factor' was crucial in marginal constituencies in the south east. 'We were finding that the reaction against Mr Kinnock was stronger the further south you got.'

Just before Mr Kinnock's own result was announced at 1.55 am, newspaper reporters started handing round copies of their first editions. These early editions went to press just before the first results came through. *The Sun* was still forecasting a possible Labour victory. Under the headline 'It's a Neil Biter' the front page splash, by political editor Trevor Kavanagh, said: 'Neil Kinnock was on the brink of walking into Number 10 last night, according to an exclusive nationwide poll for *The Sun*.' There could hardly have been a more ironic *Sun* front page: perhaps for once Mr Kinnock would have approved. However this early edition was soon superceded by other editions as the results began to pour in.

On the other side of the room the election programmes were relaying the grim reality of defeat. Mr Kinnock held Islwyn with a majority of 24 728 votes, but his victory speech sounded like a valediction. His first words were a tribute to his wife Glenys: 'In this campaign she has been the target of such spite that it disgraces those who offer it. And she bears it with a dignity that makes me proud of her as well as love her very dearly.'

There was no concession, no mention of defeat. 'The night is young,' he declared. Labour had made gains from Plymouth to Cambridge, in London, the north, the north west, Scotland and in Wales. 'The battle is not yet over,' he said. But Mr Kinnock's face told me that it was over. He had to keep up party morale for just a few hours more, that was the least he could do. But his dreams and aspirations were shattered.

His short speech pointed to one inescapable conclusion. Not only was Mr Kinnock accepting that the swing to Labour was not enough to unseat the Conservatives, but he was starting to prepare his supporters for the inevitable consequences of his second general election defeat. He was giving them the first signal that his eight-and-a-half year leadership of the party, which he turned into a personal crusade to revive the fortunes of the Labour movement, was inevitably drawing to a close.

We were all struck by the sad finality of what Mr Kinnock was saying. He said he would dedicate himself to the service of his constituents and would serve the British people 'in any capacity whatsoever.' Everyone was straining to hear his closing remarks: 'I am proud to be British and I will always be proud to serve my country.' At the far end of the room there were a couple of shouts of 'bye, bye Kinnock' and 'bye, bye loser.' But among the journalists and Conservative party workers whose actions I spent so much time observing, there was a dignified silence. We sensed that Mr Kinnock was bravely accepting that his political life was about to change.

In the space of three short hours at Conservative Central Office I witnessed a remarkable transformation. On my arrival, party workers were uneasy, with little to say. Some were clearly still fearing the worst. They seemed sure that the Conservatives would remain the largest party, but thought they might lack an overall majority. As the first results were announced they seemed puzzled by their party's good fortune, then their looks of bewilderment finally turned to glee.

Suddenly the pace of events was quickening. We were told Mr Patten was on his way back to party headquarters. A hero's welcome was promised. The prime minister's declaration was expected within the hour. Discreet preparations were already being made for the victory celebration.

My next assignment was calling me away. My task was to prepare for John Major's first day back in Downing Street and then to be on hand to report any immediate repercussions within the Labour party. I hurried back to Millbank where Labour were staging their election night reception. As I turned the corner, out of Smith Square, I kept hearing the odd cheer from the crowd behind me, as it gathered outside Central Office. Many of Labour's guests were already departing. Their sad, downcast faces reflected the bitterness of defeat. Beside me bobbing along on the pavement of Great Peter Street was a stray blue balloon, a poignant reminder of the celebrations which had barely even started just two streets away.

After the count at Islwyn Mr Kinnock returned to the party's London headquarters. He spent 40 minutes inside with campaign staff and emerged at 5.29 am with Glenys at his side, ready to concede defeat. His voice cracking with emotion, he said that they had campaigned positively and with dignity, telling the truth about the economy, poverty, the health service and education. Only Labour had the commitment to prepare the country for the challenges and realities of the future instead of leaving them to chance. 'We will work to ensure that the day will come when, with a Labour government, the country will get better in spirit, soul, and fortune and in the chances it gives to its children and in the care it gives to its infirm and elderly.'

Mr Kinnock's speech was all the stronger because he looked ahead and spoke with conviction. He remained confident that Labour was the only party capable of offering an alternative government. 'I naturally feel a strong sense of disappointment, not for myself for I am fortunate in my personal life. But I feel dismay and sorrow for so many people in our country who do not share this personal good fortune. They deserve better than they got in this election.' After returning to his home in Ealing Mr Kinnock refrained from further comment. Later, in a statement, he said he was consulting colleagues about his position and would make an announcement after the weekend. By now we all knew that his resignation was a mere formality.

FRIDAY 10 APRIL – THE DAY AFTER

John Major's triumphant return to Downing Street was a moment for the Conservatives to savour. Their fourth general election victory in a row was an achievement not matched for 150 years. At last their prime minister had his own mandate: an overall Tory majority of 21 seats secured in an election which many in his own party feared he might lose. Victory was all the sweeter because he confounded the opinion pollsters and so many of the political pundits who appeared on television and radio.

On the eve of polling day, during the final edition of *Election Call*, Mr Major acknowledged that it was time for the voters to make a judgment on his 16 months in office. Now he was his own man. The election campaign was behind him. No longer was he beholden to the news media's every whim; no longer need he be the slave of the soundbite and the deadline. Mr Major was intent on enjoying his first day back in Downing Street: it was the turn of the broadcasters to dance to his tune. We were the ones who had to sweat it out and it was our turn to struggle for words.

Mr Major's victory speech was billed as a replay of his election announcement the month before. He would emerge through the front door of Number 10 at 1.02 pm, walk over to the microphones and start speaking. Television and radio producers set to work, making all the elaborate arrangements which are necessary to ensure everything would be in place to take the prime minister's remarks live at the top of the lunchtime news bulletins and programmes.

I was assigned to *Radio Two*. A newsreader would give the headlines of the 1 pm news and then hand over to me for commentary which would fill the gap until Mr Major appeared. Unlike *Radio Four*, which was broadcasting live from Downing Street, I was reporting from a studio at Millbank, having to rely on television monitors to see what was happening.

As I began to set the scene I could see the door of Number 10 was firmly shut. A television monitor inside Number 10 was showing no sign of movement. After continuing my broadcast for several minutes, using up most of my pre-prepared information, I knew I was in danger of repeating myself. But there was still no sign of Mr Major, so I was told to hand back to the newsreader at Broadcasting House.

Other television and radio programmes faced the same dilemma. We were all forced to wait. A few more minutes elapsed without anything happening. Finally I saw Mr Major, with Mr Patten at his side, coming down the Number 10 staircase. This was the cue the newsreader was waiting for and I was told to restart my commentary. Mr Major and Mr Patten walked past the pictures and photographs of previous prime ministers. They walked together along the corridor towards the front door, stopping to talk to the Downing Street staff, who were lined up to welcome Mr Major. I kept thinking 'so far so good,' plenty of marvellous descriptive material which I could pass on to the listeners.

At last Mr Major came out through the door and into Downing

Street. However, instead of walking across to the microphones as expected, he promptly surprised us all by turning to his left. He walked off in the direction of several hundred well wishers and members of the public lined up behind barriers. As an exception they had been allowed through the security gates and into Downing Street. Mr Major was in his element, shaking hands and signing autograph books, oblivious to the plight of the broadcasters.

After keeping my commentary going for another five minutes, Mr Major was still not showing the slightest indication of walking back up Downing Street. For the second time I was told to hand back to the studio. By now our fruitless broadcast had encroached on Jimmy Young's programme time. He picked up from me with a chuckle. I could tell by his voice that it had amused him to hear me struggle to keep talking as all our carefully prepared timings went completely awry. For once Mr Major had the broadcasters on the ropes desperately searching for something new and original to say to fill the time. We were having an unexpected taste of our own medicine: the medicine we had dished out so unmercifully in the previous four weeks. We were on the spot.

Mr Major was at ease with himself. Finally, the glad handing completed, he remembered the waiting cameras and microphones. After a short speech he took questions, readily acknowledging his delight at having secured his own mandate. 'I can now accept that the country have elected me in my own right to be prime minister. I'm immensely proud of that. I shall try and ensure that I reach the aspirations of the people and that I let no one down.' The society he would work to build would be 'a truly classless society, with opportunities for all, from wherever they come, to do whatever they can with their own lives, by their own efforts and with encouragement to achieve everything that they can.'

As Mr Major and his party continued their celebrations, the savage aftermath of defeat was providing fresh drama for the election programmes. Mr Kinnock had effectively abdicated control over his party by indicating so swiftly and with such clarity his likely intention to step down. In doing so he unleashed a wave of recriminations.

Instead of retreating to lick their wounds, some Labour MPs seemed only too eager to censure the leadership and denounce the policies on which they fought the election. The whole edifice which Mr Kinnock had constructed with such care, the party unity which he fought for and which he protected with his own self discipline, was being swiftly dismantled. Rarely can a tight party machine have fallen apart so quickly.

The harshest words were from Labour MPs on the left of the party who, as promised, kept their reservations to themselves throughout the campaign. Ken Livingstone said Labour sealed their own fate. 'Once the party refused to make defence cuts, we entered a quagmire of tax and national insurance increases to pay for pensions, health and education. By expecting people on £22 000 a year to pay more, we ignored the fact that in the south east £20 000 is a typical family income.'

Mr Livingstone said that together with Tony Benn and Dennis Skinner he had agreed not to challenge party conference decisions. 'We said at the time it was wrong to water down socialism. Without defence cuts our sums would not add up without raising taxes. But anyone who dissented was stamped on and silenced. The party lost its soul and we have been soundly punished for that.'

An unexpected critic was Peter Mandelson, elected as the new Labour MP for Hartlepool. As the party's former director of communications he worked closely with Mr Kinnock in the 1987 election and contributed to remodelling Labour's image. Mr Mandelson felt the party was wrong to have raised the issue of proportional representation so close to polling day. 'This was not a strong suit for the Labour party and by igniting a long running discussion about electoral reform and hung parliaments, we deflected from our own campaign.'

However, there was trenchant criticism of some of the presentational techniques which Mr Mandelson developed on

Mr Kinnock's behalf and which were deployed to an even greater extent in the 1992 campaign. Kim Howells, MP for Pontypridd, said party members were sickened by the glitzy, show biz nonsense Labour indulged in. 'This triumphalism, where people leapt on to stages trying to look like pop stars and actors, is not what voters want. There is no substitute for slogging around the streets, talking to people and getting the message across.'

All talk of a hung parliament evaporated the moment the election night programmes started predicting an overall majority for Mr Major. By pushing their share of the vote comfortably above the level predicted by the opinion polls, the Conservatives easily retook seats lost to the Liberal Democrats in by elections at Eastbourne, Ribble Valley and Kincardine and Deeside. Paddy Ashdown had the consolation of spectacular gains in Bath and Cheltenham, but overall his parliamentary party was reduced to twenty, a net loss of two MPs.

At their post-election news conference there were no recrimina-tions. If the election had been conducted under a system of propor-tional representation the Liberal Democrats' 18.3% share of the vote would have translated into 108 seats at Westminster. Mr Ashdown praised the contribution of Des Wilson who took on the job of campaign director when the Liberal Democrats share of support in the opinion polls stood at only 6%. 'People said we would be wiped out, but Des ensured we won the argument. I could not have coped in the last three months without his help and steadfastness.' Mr Wilson blamed the unelectability of Labour for scaring away potential supporters. 'Our campaign reached its peak on Monday. But the message that the Tories kept hammering home, that a vote for the Liberal Democrats was a vote for Labour, did damage us in the closing stages.'

Tory newspapers made great play of Mr Major's claim that the Liberal Democrats would let Mr Kinnock into Downing Street. This was taken up by the *Daily Express* on the last day of the campaign. Under the headline 'Don't Throw it All Away' the front page showed a picture of a Trojan horse. Its head was a representation of Mr Ashdown's face and inside the horse was Mr Kinnock.

The newspaper front page which caused Labour the greatest anger was printed by *The Sun* on polling day. Superimposed on a picture of a light bulb was a photograph of Mr Kinnock's face. Alongside the illustration was the following headline: 'If Kinnock wins today, will the last person to leave Britain please turn out the lights.' A caption to the illustration said that if the next prime minister ended up being 'a bald bloke with wispy red hair and two K's in his surname, we'll see you at the aiport.'

Television news reports from Basildon, which was attracting publicity because of its role as a barometer of marginal constituencies, showed *Sun* front pages being displayed by Conservative supporters on polling day. David Hart, a former aide to Mrs Thatcher told me the inspiration for the 'light bulb' splash and Wednesday's eight page spread 'Nightmare on Kinnock Street' came from *The Sun's* editor Kelvin MacKenzie. 'Kelvin wanted *The Sun* to have two really punchy editions on the last two days of the campaign. His strategy was superb. They were brilliant examples of political propaganda. What we saw was the tabloids come out in front of the party, develop their own line and take a lead in popularising the Conservatives.

David Hill expressed Labour's outrage. He believed the heavy concentration of anti-Labour bias in newspapers like *The Sun* had a significant impact on floating voters in the final few days. Labour failed to take some of its target seats by the merest of margins: there were nine constituencies where Labour were beaten by Conservative candidates with majorities of less than 300 votes. Four of the seats stayed Tory on majorities of less than 100 votes, for example, Hayes and Harlington remained Tory by the skin of its teeth, with a majority of 53, and Bristol North West's Tory majority was reduced to mere 45. Mr Hill said the desperate smear tactics of the Tory newspapers could well have influenced undecided voters. 'There was what I can only describe as the most vituperative attack on any political party that I have ever seen, and it came from the tabloid press.'

The importance of the press campaign against Labour was subsequently underlined by Lord McAlpine, a former treasurer to the Conservative party. In his campaign notebook for the *Sunday Telegraph* on 12 April, he accused Central Office of greatly under-estimating the influence of the tabloid newspapers. Lord McAlpine considered the heroes of the election were Sir David English, Sir Nicholas Lloyd and Kelvin MacKenzie, respectively the editors of the *Daily Mail*, the *Daily Express*, and *The Sun*. 'Never in the past nine elections have they come out so strongly in favour of the Conservatives. Never has their attack on the Labour party been so comprehensive. They exposed, ridiculed and humiliated that party, doing each day in their pages the job that the politicians failed to do from their bright new platforms. This was how the election was won, and if the politicians, elated in their hour of victory, are tempted to believe otherwise, they are in very real trouble next time.'

I met Lord McAlpine at several Conservative news conferences. On Wednesday 1 April, the day of Labour's seven point opinion poll lead, he was contemplating possible tactics. He recalled how after a similar setback in the last election, when he was party treasurer, the Conservatives ordered a massive newspaper advertising campaign to bolster Tory fortunes. 'What we did after "wobbly Thursday" in 1987 when we were also hit by adverse polling figures, was to blitz the press with full page advertisements. I wonder what device they'll use in this election?' I thought then that the Conservatives probably lacked the financial resources to repeat the same kind of saturation advertising. Judging by Lord McAlpine's *Sunday Telegraph* campaign diary, he obviously considered that the editorial space devoted to boosting the Tory campaign by the tabloids had proved even more effective in the end than any advertising campaign.

As Labour MPs and party strategists began to argue over the mistakes and failures of their campaign, I found it unsettling to see replays on television news bulletins of Mr Kinnock's speech conceding defeat. The all or nothing finality of the British electoral system can be terribly cruel. A tired, beaten leader has to find some way to rally and inspire a dejected party.

Mr Kinnock had delivered a moving, forceful restatement of everything he had fought for. But within 12 hours of defeat, senior members of the shadow cabinet were lining themselves up for a leadership election. Close friends said that Mr Kinnock had simply had enough: he wanted the contest to choose his successor to start as soon as possible.

All day the image of Mr Kinnock's strained, taught face haunted me. I had witnessed similar devastation so often before on the faces of trade union leaders crushed under Mrs Thatcher. As labour correspondent for BBC radio throughout the 1980s I reported on defeat after defeat in the union movement. The policies pursued by Mrs Thatcher's governments undermined and then destroyed the strength and unity of collective industrial action.

I was reminded of those defeats when Mrs Thatcher congratulated Mr Major and their party on the Conservatives fourth successive election victory. She felt her legacy was safe. 'Everything we have done in the last 13 years will now be conserved and built on into the future. People weren't prepared to let those achievements go.'

Decline in workplace solidarity, falling strike figures and the continued retreat of the unions remain as testiminonies to Mrs Thatcher's years in office. Her policies have eaten away at another tenet of the Labour movement: their belief in the principle of a redistributive tax system, which transfers money from the rich to the poor.

As Labour began its post-election inquest, there was considerable criticism of the shadow budget and their misplaced belief that enough of the electorate would support a manifesto promising tax increases. Mr Kinnock was troubled throughout the election campaign by the likely unpopularity of their plans, and especially the proposal to increase national insurance for those on higher incomes. He spoke frequently and passionately of the need to end poverty, but avoided saying he wanted to clobber the rich.

As I watched those haunting images, again and again, of Mr Kinnock conceding defeat, I felt that he was a victim of the Thatcher era. He was a trade union member, he was their man, he was a creature of the power of the union block vote. He had tried so hard to ensure that his party came to terms with the Thatcher revolution, but being a creature of the very people who were swept aside by that revolution, he inevitably became the Thatcher revolution's final victim.